YOUR RIGHTS TO SOCIAL SECURITY BENEFITS

YOUR RIGHTS TO SOCIAL SECURITY BENEFITS

DAVID ANDREWS

Facts On File, Inc.
460 Park Avenue South, New York, N.Y. 10016

YOUR RIGHTS TO SOCIAL SECURITY BENEFITS

© Copyright 1981 by Andrews Publishing Co.

Published by Facts On File, Inc., 460 Park Avenue South, New York, N.Y. 10016

All rights reserved. No part of this book may be reproduced in any form whatever without the express written consent of the publisher except for reasonably brief extracts used in reviews or scholarly works.

Library of Congress Cataloging in Publication Data

Andrews, David, 1941-
   Your Rights to Social Security Benefits

   Includes index.
   1. Social Security—United States—Miscellanea.
I. Title.
HD7125 .A58　　　　　　344.73'023　　　　　　81-9787
ISBN O-87196-600-X　　　347.30423　　　　　　AACR2
ISBN O-87196-601-8 (pbk)
Printed and bound in the United States of America
9 8 7 6 5 4 3 2 1

CONTENTS

Social Security: What, Why, How and How Much 1
   Questions and Answers 7
Collecting Benefits 13
   Questions and Answers 24
Retirement Benefits 32
   Questions and Answers 38
Disability Benefits 43
   Questions and Answers 53
Survivors' Benefits 69
   Questions and Answers 75
Supplemental Security Income 81
   Questions and Answers 93
Medicare 96
   Questions and Answers: General 105
Medicare: Part A 109
   Questions and Answers: Part A 115
Medicare: Part B 125
   Questions and Answers: Part B 132
Limits of Medicare 149
Additional Notes and Special Cases 156
   Questions and Answers: Special Cases 170
   Other Questions and Answers 179
Index 183

SOCIAL SECURITY: WHAT, WHY, HOW AND HOW MUCH

We take it for granted today, as though it had always been there. But Social Security is a relatively recent innovation, not even 50 years old. In 1935, President Franklin D. Roosevelt signed the Social Security Act and ushered in a new era in society's concern for the average citizen and the quality of his life.

It was not a new idea. Government-sponsored old-age and sickness insurance programs had been attempted in Germany in the 1800s. But in America it was an idea whose time had come. The country was in the middle of a severe nationwide economic depression. There were breadlines and soup kitchens in the streets. Thousands of newly homeless Americans lived in tar-paper shacks. Hard-working people who felt secure in their savings had seen everything wiped out by the stock market crash and bank failures. For millions it was like starting over.

Roosevelt pushed for a government-sponsored insurance program that could provide some security for workers who had lost all sense of security. The Act that he signed toward the end of his first term in office would be one of his most enduring achievements. Social Security has become as certain as . . . taxes.

That's how it was to be funded, through a special tax that workers covered by Social Security would pay during their earning years and collect in retirement or in the case of disability.

Ida Fuller, a bookkeeper from Vermont, received the first retirement check in 1940. The amount of the check was $22.54. With her first check alone, Ida Fuller exceeded the amount of her contribution, which was only $22. And she lived to be over 100 years old, collecting more than $22,000 in Social Security benefits along the way.

In 1940, Ida Fuller was one of less than a quarter of a million people who collected the first benefits from Social Security. Today, more than 36 million people are collecting benefits from Social Security, at least half of them under 65, and 116 million contribute to the program. About 90 per cent of Americans will, at some time in their lives, be eligible for benefits under the Social Security program.

Social Security has gone through many changes since 1935. Methods of financing have had to be revised and payments have changed dramatically. One of the most dramatic changes was the adjustment in the Social Security law linking benefit payments to rises in the cost of living. If the cost-of-living index rises more than three per cent in any year, Social Security benefit recipients will get a compensatory increase in benefits. The increase for 1981 alone will be 11.2 per cent.

There had been a great deal of debate during the past few years about the continuing effectiveness of Social Security and whether or not American workers could continue to pay for such a far-reaching plan. But additional tax revenues have made the system solvent for at least the near future.

From 1968 through 1977, the level of benefits increased by about 130 per cent. And with the automatic increases legislated, current workers paying for the program have even brighter future benefits. Changes in the law and contribution schedules have made Social Security more expensive today than ever in the past, but those increased payments will reap even greater future benefits.

WHO IS NOT COVERED

Although nine out of ten workers become eligible for Social Security benefits, some people are *not* covered. This includes those who work for a non-profit organization that has decided not to join Social Security; ministers, priests, rabbis, or Christian Science practitioners who have chosen not to be included and who do not pay Social Security taxes on their earnings; workers in a state, local, or Federal government division that has its own pension system and is not included in Social Security; people working outside the United States for a foreign government, foreign company, or international organization; people who live on inheritances, dividends, capital gains or real estate rental incomes; railroad workers, who have a separate retirement system that is run in conjuction with Social Security; and Presidents of the United States, who do not contribute to the system and are not covered.

CREDITS FOR BENEFITS

For most working people, the required number of credits to be "fully insured" come as a matter of course. But occasionally, people work for periods of time in jobs that are not covered by Social Security and then find that they have not enough credits to collect benefits from Social Security. You earn credits on a quarterly basis each year. The basis is fully explained in the next chapter, but if you are short of credits for benefits, the missing credits can be made up at any time, even after you turn 65. Some ways to earn credits are through part-time and temporary jobs and self-employment. As little as $400 in income during a year can make you eligible for self-employed work credits. You cannot, however, receive work credits if you work for your husband or wife or son or daughter and he or she is the sole owner of a business or profession. If the business is a partnership with a partner who is not a close relative, you *can* receive credit. And if the business is a corporation, you *can* receive credit, whoever is the owner.

If you have worked in a job that is not covered under Social Security and you are eligible for retirement benefits from that job, you can earn enough work credits to also collect Social Security benefits. And Social Security benefits are not affected by any other income from pensions or savings.

DISABILITY PROTECTION

In addition to retirement benefits, you become eligible for disability benefits under Social Security only 18 months after you start to work. As long as you remain at least "currently insured" you continue to have this protection which is more fully explained in the "Disability Benefits" chapter of this book.

WIVES AND HUSBANDS OF INSURED WORKERS

Wives and husbands of insured workers are entitled to collect 50 per cent of their spouse's retirement benefits when they reach retirement age if they do not have their own Social Security work credits. The benefits a spouse collects are in addition to the retirement benefits the worker receives.

Benefits are slightly reduced if the wife or husband chooses to start collecting at age 62 instead of waiting until he or she becomes 65.

A spouse can collect this percentage of a worker's retirement benefits even if they are divorced—and even if the worker has remarried—as long as their marriage lasted at least ten years.

SURVIVOR'S INSURANCE

The value of the survivor's insurance benefits under Social Security have been estimated at well over $100,000. This coverage is invaluable for any family. See the chapter on Survivor's Benefits for full information.

CONFIDENTIALITY

Social Security is not permitted to reveal any information it might have about you to relatives, friends, employers, neighbors, banks or anyone else. The law prohibits any such disclosure except information needed by the Federal government in a law enforcement matter, or to locate a person who is liable for his children's support. Social Security may also give information about you to a hospital official if the information is to be used for your medical benefit. Social Security will not even reveal your real age to your husband or wife. And the Administration will go so far in keeping your secret that it will even send separate checks to a husband or wife on request.

DIRECT DEPOSIT

You may have benefits from Social Security deposited directly into your account at a commercial or savings bank, savings and loan association, Federal or state credit union, or other similar institution.

To arrange for direct deposit, all you have to do is complete a direct deposit form SF-1199. You can get the form at your financial organization. Your monthly benefit check contains all the information you'll need for the direct deposit form.

Completion of the form only authorizes deposits into your account. Only you or someone authorized by you can make withdrawals from your account.

Direct deposit of your checks will start about 90 days after Social Security gets the form SF-1199 from your financial organization. Many financial organizations notify their customers when direct depositing of their checks starts. In the meantime, you continue to receive checks at home.

If you ever want to change from one financial organization to another, just fill out a new form SF-1199 at the new financial organization. You can stop direct deposit at any time simply by notifying your Social Security office.

THE RECORDS YOU NEED

When you go to a Social Security office, you should bring your Social Security card or your number. Whenever you apply for benefits you will have to show who you are, your age and your relationship to any other person on whose record you might collect benefits or who might collect benefits on your record.

Bring these records or documents if they have any bearing on your case: spouse's Social Security card or record of the number; proof of age (your own and spouse's); marriage certificate; birth certificate for children who are to receive benefits; certified adoption order if child is adopted; death certificate of worker who has died; receipted funeral bill, if you are claiming the lump sum death benefit and are neither the widow and widower of the deceased worker; death papers; military discharge or statement of service, if you are a veteran; your latest income tax withholding statement (W-2 form). Your latest tax return, if you are self-employed.

QUESTIONS AND ANSWERS

Question: What is Social Security?

Answer: Social Security is the American version of a concept of government sponsored social insurance that dates at least to the late 19th century, when Germany introduced old-age and sickness insurance. The United States program, begun under the Social Security Act of 1935 under President Franklin D. Roosevelt, subsidizes old-age (retirement), disability and health insurance for 90 per cent of the country's work force and their families.

Question: How does the program work?

Answer: Employees, their employers, and self-employed people all are required to make Social Security contributions, which are put into special trust funds. When a worker retires, becomes disabled or dies, he and his dependents or his survivors receive monthly cash benefits—social insurance—from the trust funds. Part of the contributions is used to finance the hospital-insurance program under Medicare (Medicare is the health-insurance branch of the Social Security program).

Question: What determines the size of my contribution?

Answer: Your contribution is determined by the earnings you get from work that is covered by Social Security. If you are employed, your contribution (6.65 per cent) is deducted from your salary, and your employer pays an equal amount. If you are self-employed, you pay 9.3 per cent for retirement, survivor's and disability insurance, and hospital insurance.

Question: Will contributions continue to be deducted from my salary no matter how much I earn in a year?

Answer: No. After your earnings reach a certain maximum amount, no more Social Security deductions will be made for that year. (Of course, you're free to keep on earning as much as you want to or are able to after you've passed the maximum—the maximum is a retriction on the Social Security program, not you! In 1981, the maximum will be $29,700. And for history buffs, the maximum was $25,900 in 1980; $17,700 in 1978; $16,500 in 1977; $15,300 in 1976; $14,100 in 1975; $13,200 in 1974; $10,800 in 1973; $9,000 in 1972; $7,800 in 1968-71; $6,600 in 1966 and 1967; $4,800 in 1959-65; $4,200 in 1955-58; $3,600 in 1951-54, and $3,000 in 1937-1950. In percentage terms, the contribution rate for 1981 is 6.65 per cent. In dollar terms, people earning $29,700 or more will pay a total contribution of $1,975.00 in 1981 while a middle-income worker earning $15,000 will pay $994.50.

Question: Someone must have thought Social Security was a good thing if it's been in effect since 1935 and if there's no way I can stop my contributions. But I wonder—wouldn't I come out ahead if the money I lose to Social Security in every paycheck right now was put instead into one of my savings accounts, or if I was allowed to invest it myself?

Answer: It has been estimated that most people would have to have more than $100,000 in cash, stocks and bonds, or in a savings account earning 5 percent interest, to equal what they could receive under Social Security. And don't forget that Social Security benefits are tax-free, unlike the interest on the money in a savings account, and unlike the stocks and bonds when they are converted to cash. If you retire in 1981 and you paid in the maximum contribution for all the years since 1937 when the Social Security Administration began collecting taxes, you would have paid a total of $14,865.69. The maximum benefit payable to an individual is $653.80 per month. Therefore, in about 20 months you would receive in benefits all the money that you put into the system. Of course, if you were receiving the family maximum of $1143.70 per month, you would receive back in less than one year the total amount of your contribution.

Question: Don't most people benefit from other pension plans in addition to Social Security?

Answer: No. For slightly more than half of the country's labor force, Social Security benefits are the sole source of retirement income.

Question: What determines how much I'll be getting in retirement or disability benefits?

Answer: The amount is based on your average earnings, for a certain period of years, for work covered by Social Security. The same applies to benefits your dependents or survivors may receive.

Question: What kinds of work are covered by Social Security?

Answer: Virtually all kinds of employment and self-employment are covered. However, there are special rules for some occupations, so you should contact your Social Security office if any of the following apply to you—(1) you are less than 21 years old and work for a parent; (2) you work for your spouse; (3) you work in your child's home; (4) you work in or about your employer's private home; (5) you are a student employed at a school; (6) you are a farm worker; (7) you get cash tips; or (8) you work for a state or local government, a non-profit or international organization.

Question: One look at my grocery bill and I can see that the cost of living has gone nowhere but up. Are Social Security benefits going to keep pace with inflation?

Answer: Beginning in 1975, benefits rise automatically when the Consumer Price Index rises 3 per cent or more. In 1980 the cost of living increase applied to benefits being received was 14.3 per cent.

Question: How can I get a Social Security card?

Answer: You can apply at your nearest Social Security office. Be sure to bring proof of your age, identity, and citizenship or alien status.

Question: I have nothing to hide, but will my Social Security records be kept confidential?

Answer: Yes. Information about you from your records cannot, by law, be disclosed without proper authorization.

Question: Now that I've got my Social Security card, what do I use if for?

Answer: First, sign it. Show it to any employer you have if your work is covered by Social Security. And keep it handy for income-tax purposes. Anyone who pays you interest, dividends or other income that must be reported on your tax return may want your Social Security number.

Question: Someone told me I should tattoo my Social Security number on my body to make sure I'd never forget what it was. Is this a good idea?

Answer: Your one Social Security number must last you a lifetime, so if you have trouble remembering your zip code and seem to lose small items habitually, you may find yourself considering a tattoo. But remember that Medicare cannot pay for tattooing and that there is the initial risk of infection.

Question: I've lost my Social Security card. What do I do?

Answer: Apply for a duplicate at your Social Security office. (Bring with you two pieces of identification.) You will get a new card, but not a new number.

Question: I think my card has been stolen. Should I tell the police or Social Security?

Answer: Apply for a new card at your Social Security office. You will receive a duplicate of the original card—not a new number. If your card was in your wallet along with other valuables when it was stolen, or if your card and your wallet were in your car when the car was stolen, perhaps you should call the police.

Question: My named changed when I got married, and my sister changed her name when she started attending drama school. Do we need new Social Security cards?

Answer: Yes. Your Social Security office will get you new cards bearing your new names and your old numbers. Since you've just been married, now you know the meaning of "something old, something new."

Question: I can't get to a Social Security office in person, but I'd like to talk to someone from the office. Can this be arranged?

Answer: Yes. If you are hospitalized or unable to leave home, and your problem can't be discussed easily by telephone, a Social Security representative will visit you.

Question: We live in a small community and the nearest Social Security office is an inconvenient distance away. How can we get our questions answered?

Answer: You can telephone or write any Social Security office (there are 1,200 in the United States). In addition, representatives make regular visits to 3,500 communities like yours. You can get information about the next visit to your area by contacting the nearest Social Security office. The telephone number is listed under "Social Security Administration" and under "United States Government—Health and Human Services, Dept. of." If you don't have a telephone, ask at your post office.

Question: How can I be sure my Social Security records are correct? I've never even seen them.

Answer: Your records are kept at the headquarters of the Social Security Administration, in Baltimore. To find out if your taxable wages and self-employment earnings have been recorded accurately, call or visit your Social Security office and ask for the Social Security postcard known as the "Request for Statement of Earnings." Mail the card to the headquarters and you will receive by return mail your confidential Social Security report.

Question: Should I be checking my records regularly, or can I trust Social Security to get everything right?

Answer: You should be checking. Some employers in the past have neglected to forward the Social Security taxes they withheld from their employees' paychecks. If this happened to you, your record would not give you credit for the work you did and the taxes you paid. And errors in bookkeeping are always possible. So you should be checking, at least every other year if possible, because you have only about three years from the time an error is made to correct it.

Question: I overheard two men in a bar say they were going to bilk Social Security by getting two or more Social Security numbers each. What happens if they get caught?

Answer: Criminal prosecutions and convictions for fraud can result in fines of between $500 and $10,000 or imprisonment of from 1 to 15 years.

Question: I'd like more information about Social Security. How can I get it?

Answer: You can always contact your Social Security office and talk to a staff member. Or you can phone or write or stop in at the office to collect any of a number of free pamphlets dealing with all aspects of the program. If the stocks are deplete, you can request the pamphlets from the Social Security Administration, Office of Public Affairs, 6401 Security Boulevard, Baltimore, MD 21235.

COLLECTING BENEFITS

YOU HAVE TO APPLY

To collect any benefits you must get in touch with Social Security first. There are Social Security offices conveniently located throughout the United States. And the people who staff these offices are generally knowledgeable, concerned and helpful. But by its nature, Social Security does not come to you and say that you have money coming. You must contact Social Security.

Look up the closest office under "Social Security" in the white pages of your telephone book. Call your local office, give your Social Security number, and ask for information. They can usually answer questions of a general nature or about specific benefits right away. If you want to find out about your current status in Social Security, you can request a card to be mailed to Social Security's central office which will be returned to you with the information on your earnings record.

YOUR EARNINGS RECORD

If you've ever worked in a job covered by Social Security, the Social Security Administration has an individual lifetime earnings record for you at its headquarters in Baltimore, Maryland. Year after year, as long as your work is covered by Social Security, reports of your earnings are sent to Baltimore and the computer adds the amounts to your record.

Your Social Security earnings record is important. When you or your family applies for benefits your record will be checked to see if you worked long enough for benefits to be payable and how much benefits will be.

YOUR EARNINGS STATEMENT

Your earnings statement shows the earnings listed to you in the Social Security records beginning with 1937. It includes your wages from employment and any self-employment income which you report each year as a part of your individual income tax return.

Your latest earnings may not be shown on the statement. In the past, earnings were reported to the Social Security Administration on a quarterly basis. Now, earnings are reported annually, after the end of the year. Because of this and because of the time it will take to credit all the earnings reported to individual reports, the two latest years' earnings may not be shown on your record.

As wages were not covered for Social Security purposes until 1937, no earnings prior to that time are shown. And no earnings for self-employment can be credited before 1951.

ELIGIBILITY FOR BENEFITS

You might believe that Social Security benefits are automatically coming to you just because you have a Social Security number. Unfortunately, that isn't the case.

While most people who are in the Social Security system and working *are* covered, you must qualify for benefits. To qualify, you must contribute to Social Security for a certain length of time.

These periods of time are recorded as credits which are made to your Social Security account. All of the work you do that is covered by Social Security is credited to your account but you must accumulate enough work credits to collect any benefits.

Once you have accumulated enough credits to qualify, you are eligible from then on for at least the minimum in benefits.

WHAT ARE WORK CREDITS?

You earn a work credit whenever you receive $310 for work covered by Social Security in a year. The maximum number of credits you may earn in any year is four. These work credits were once (before 1978) called work quarters and were considered earned only if the required minimum was earned during each three-month period starting in January. Since then, however, the requirements have been changed and once you earn at least $1,240 within a calendar year, you have earned four work credits for that year, whether the income is earned in a week, a month, or over the entire year.

HOW MANY WORK CREDITS ARE NEEDED?

To be eligible for retirement benefits, you must have 29 work credits if you turn 62 in 1981. If you reach 62 in 1983, you need 32 credits. By 1987 you must have 36 credits and after 1991, 40 work credits will be required as a minimum necessity for Social Security retirement benefits.

Once you earn the required number of credits you have full coverage for life, even though you may quit working before you reach retirement age. But the amount of your benefits is based on an average of the earnings covered under Social Security during the time you were employed.

Most people have no trouble earning the necessary credits. If you work regularly in jobs covered by Social Security you will eventually be fully covered and be eligible to collect benefits.

There are millions of people, however, who cannot collect Social Security benefits because they might work a few years and build up some Social Security credits and then they stop working to get married and raise a family or they change to a job that isn't covered. These people throw away everything they paid into Social Security and they subsequently lose thousands of dollars in future benefits.

There are alternatives.

To begin, before you make any major changes in your employment, figure out the number of work credits you have already in your Social Security account. Call the Social Security office near you and they will send you a free postcard to mail as an inquiry to headquarters. You will get it back with an up-to-date statement of the number of work credits in your account.

Deduct the amount of work credits that Social Security shows in your account from the requirement. Any remainder must still be earned in order for you to be fully insured.

EXTRA CREDITS FOR MILITARY SERVICE

Remember to include any military service in your calculations. In additional to the normal credit for military wages covered under Social Security, you can also receive extra earnings credit.

If you were on active military service between 1957 and 1977, you can receive extra earnings credits of $300 for each calendar quarter that you served. From 1978 on, you can receive additional earnings credits of $100 for every $300 in annual military salary covered by Social Security up to a maximum of $1,200 in extra credits for the year.

If you saw active military duty between September 15, 1940 through 1956, you may also be awarded additional earnings credits of $160 a month.

These extra earnings credits will not be listed on your earnings statement. If it should be found that these credits make you eligible for a higher payment, Social Security will ask you to supply your service record.

If you served before 1957, you probably will not be allowed to use your military service to apply for Social Security benefits *and* military pensions.

SELF-EMPLOYMENT FOR SOCIAL SECURITY BENEFITS

Nearly all self-employment is covered by social security. You're self-employed if you engage in a trade, business, or profession, either by yourself or as a partner. You report your earnings for Social Security at the time you file your Federal income tax return.

SELF-EMPLOYMENT EARNINGS

You get Social Security credit for your earnings if your net earnings from self-employment amount to $400 or more in a year. You may get credit even if your net income is less than $400, using an optional method of reporting earnings.

When your net earnings are $400 or more in a year, you get Social Security credit for all your earnings up to the maximum that counts for Social Security, $29,700 for 1981.

The amount of your future Social Security benefits depends on the amount of your earnings. So, it's important for you to report all your earnings up to the maximum. It is also required by law.

If you have wages as well as self-employment earnings, the wages count first for Social Security. If your wages are less than the Social Security maximum, you pay the self-employment tax only on the difference between your wages and the maximum, or on your net earnings if less. The self-employment tax rate is 9.3 percent for 1981.

Getting to the Net

Your net earnings for Social Security are your gross earnings from your profession, trade, or business minus your business deductions and depreciation. If you have more than one business, combine the profit or loss from all of them when you figure your net earnings.

The following kinds of income don't count for Social Security:
Dividends from shares of stock and interest on bonds or other

instruments issued by corporations, unless you receive them as a dealer in stocks and securities.

Interest from loans, unless your business is lending money.

Rentals from real estate, unless you are a real estate dealer or you regularly furnish services mostly for the convenience of the occupant. Real estate dealers should count income only from properties held as stock in trade.

Income received by a limited partner if you don't perform services for the partnership.

The Option

If your actual net is less than $400, you can still get Social Security credit under the optional method mentioned earlier if your gross profit is $600 or more. The option can also be used in many cases when your net profit is less than $1,600.

You can use the optional method only if your actual net has been $400 or more in at least two of the last three years. You can use the optional method no more than five times, and it may be used only if net earnings are less than two-thirds of your gross income. It cannot be used to report earnings less than actual net earnings.

How to Figure the Optional Method

If your gross income is between $600 and $2,400, you may report two-thirds of your gross or your actual net earnings if $400 or more.

If your gross income is $2,400 or more and actual net earnings are $1,600, you must report your actual net earnings.

Partners can also use the option. Generally, the partnership gross income is divided on the same basis as profit or loss and allocated to the partners for purposes of the option.

Reporting Your Earnings

After any year in which you have net earnings of $400 or more, complete Form 1040 (U.S. Individual Income Tax Return), Schedule C (Profit or Loss from Business or Profession), and

Schedule SE (Computation of Social Security Self-Employment Tax).

You can get these forms from the Internal Revenue Service or at banks and post offices.

Send the tax return and schedules, along with your self-employment tax, to the Internal Revenue Service on or before April 15 of the following year.

Estimating Taxes

On or before April 15 of any year for which you expect to owe $100 or more in income taxes and self-employment tax, you may have to file a declaration of estimated tax on Form 1040-ES and pay the estimated tax or the first installment.

Social Security and Income Tax

Social Security taxes may be due even though you don't owe any income tax. As long as your income is subject to the Social Security tax, you must file your Federal tax return and pay the Social Security tax. This is true even if you get Social Security benefits.

Be sure to show your Social Security number on all forms. Do not use your employer identification number in place of your Social Security number when reporting your own earnings.

Self-Employed Husbands and Wives

If you and your husband or wife operate a business as a true partnership or joint venture, you each report your share of the business profits as net earnings on separate schedules, even though you file a joint income tax return. The amount each of you should report depends on your agreement. Each of you will get Social Security credit if each has net earnings of $400 or more.

If you aren't actual partners, net earnings go only to the one who manages and controls the business. This usually is the husband; and the net earnings should be reported for him alone, even if you file a joint income tax return. In a community-property state, the earnings are considered the husband's unless the wife exercises practically all management and control of the business.

Other Family Members

A parent and child may be partners or joint venturers. In either case, both are self-employed and each should report his or her share of the business profits as net earnings.

Employees of Foreign Governments

A special rule applies to the United States citizens working in this country for a foreign government, an international organization, or an instrumentality wholly owned by a foreign government.

You must report your earnings from these employers as though you were self-employed. You include a separate Schedule SE with your Federal income tax return and pay Social Security self-employment taxes on your earnings.

RAILROAD WORKERS

Railroad workers have a separate retirement system operated by the Railroad Retirement Board, 844 Rush Street, Chicago, Illinois 60611. Your Social Security earnings statement does not include any money you have earned from a railroad.

EARNINGS FOR SOCIAL SECURITY CREDIT

The maximum amount of earnings in any one year which can be used to figure Social Security benefits is set by the law. The following table shows the maximum amount for each year from 1937 through 1981.

The maximum applies to the combined amount of wages and self-employment income for a taxable year.

Starting with 1982, the amount of yearly earnings that count for Social Security will increase automatically to keep pace with increases in average wage levels.

ANNUAL MAXIMUM   FOR EACH YEAR

$ 3,000	1937 through 1950
3,600	1951 through 1954
4,200	1955 through 1958
4,800	1959 through 1965
6,600	1966 and 1967
7,800	1968 through 1971
9,000	1972
10,800	1973
13,200	1974
14,100	1975
15,300	1976
16,500	1977
17,700	1978
22,900	1979
25,900	1980
29,700	1981

If amounts above the maximum for a year were reported to your record, they may be included in the statement of earnings you get from Social Security. But no more than the maximum can be used to figure benefits.

TAXES

Your statement of earnings shows only the earnings reported for you. It does not show the amount of the Social Security taxes you or your employer paid. Benefits under the retirement, survivors, and disability insurance programs are figured from your earnings covered by the law, not from the taxes paid. Therefore, it is not possible to pay in extra taxes with the hope of getting higher benefits later on.

REFUNDS

If you work for more than one employer in any year and pay Social Security taxes on more than the maximum amount, you may claim a refund on these excess taxes on your income tax return for that year.

IF YOU DISAGREE

If your own record of your earnings does not agree with the amount shown in the earnings statement you get from Social Security, call, write, or visit your Social Security office promptly. Give your Social Security number, the periods of employment involved, wages paid you in each period, and the employer's name and address. If you have W-2 forms (Wage and Tax Statement), pay slips, or other proof of unrecorded wages, include them when you contact the office.

If the earnings in question were from self-employment, include the date you filed your report and the location of the Internal Revenue Service office to which the report was sent. Submit copies of your tax returns for the years not recorded, along with canceled checks (if you have them), showing payment of the contributions.

MINIMUM BENEFITS

There is a special minimum benefit at retirement for some people who worked under Social Security at least 20 years. This helps people who had low earnings, still above a specified level, in their working years. The amount of the special minimum depends on the number of years of coverage. For a worker retiring at 65 with 30 or more years of coverage in 1980, the minimum would be $289. Most people who have worked 20 years or more under Social Security already receive benefits higher than the special minimum.

Years of coverage from 1937 to 1950 are determined by dividing the total covered wages for those years by $900, with a maximum of 14 years of coverage counted for that period. After 1950, a year of coverage is any year a person has earnings of at least 25 per cent of the maximum covered by Social Security.

The special minimum benefit will be increased automatically in future years as the cost of living rises.

CREDIT FOR DELAYED RETIREMENT

A worker who reaches 65 before 1982 will receive an increase of 1 per cent for each year ($\frac{1}{12}$ of 1 per cent for each month) from age 65 to 72 that he or she didn't get benefits.

Workers who reach 65 in 1982 or later will get 3 per cent for each year ($\frac{1}{4}$ of 1 per cent for each month) from age 65 to 72 that they don't get benefits.

This credit will apply even though a worker received reduced benefits before age 65.

The worker's delayed retirement credit also will be applied to the benefit payable to a worker's widow or widower.

QUESTIONS AND ANSWERS

Question: How much work do I have to do to qualify for Social Security benefits?

Answer: To begin with, what you consider a year of work may not always be what the Social Security program considers a year of work. So it helps to know what is meant when someone says, for example, "He gets credit for four years of work." Most employees get credit for one-quarter year of work if they receive $260 or more in covered wages in a three-month calendar quarter. If a person is self-employed, or works at one job but is also self-employed, his income is covered under Social Security if he has a net profit of $400 or more. He earns one quarter of coverage for each $310 of his covered self-employment income up to a maximum of four quarters per year. A farm worker gets credit if he receives at least $150 in cash pay from one employer during a year or he is employed on 20 or more days during a year for cash pay figured on a time basis (by the hour, day, week) regardless of the amount of pay. He gets one quarter of coverage for each $310 of covered earnings up to a maximum of four quarters per year. The wages of a domestic employee in a private household are covered if he or she is paid $50 or more in cash in a three-month calendar quarter by one employer. A quarter of coverage is earned for each $310 of covered wages, up to a maximum of four quarters in one year. So whether you can say, for Social Security purposes, that you worked 10 years, or five years, or just a year and a half, depends on whether you earned the prescribed amount in a prescribed period of time.

Secondly, there are two ways to be insured under Social Security. You can be "currently insured" or "fully insured." You are "currently insured" if you have Social Security credit for at least one-and-a-half years of work during the three years before you become entitled to retirement benefits or die.

COLLECTING BENEFITS

Whether you are "fully insured" depends on the year in which you reach 62 years of age, or become disabled, or die. It also depends on how much work credit you have. A chart follows:

Year you reach 62, die or become disabled	Amount of work credit you need to be fully insured
1974	6*
1975	6
1976	6¼
1977	6½
1978	6¾
1979	7
1981	7½
1983	8
1987	9
1991 or later	10

*For 1974, a woman needed only 5¾.

Question: Other than the different work requirements, what's the difference between being currently insured and fully insured?

Answer: People who are fully insured are eligible for more kinds of cash benefits than are people who are only currently insured. However, being fully insured does not necessarily mean your payments will be larger than the payments of those who are only currently insured. To illustrate:

RETIREMENT BENEFITS

Who will get monthly payments?	Insured status you must have
You, as a retired worker, and your wife and children, and in some cases your former wife or surviving former wife	Fully insured

Your husband age 60 or older	Fully insured
Widow 60 or older, or disabled widow, 50 or older, and in some cases your wife or surviving former wife	Fully insured
Widow of any age if caring for child who is less than 18 or disabled and entitled to benefits, and in some cases your former wife or surviving former wife	Fully or currently insured
A widower of any age caring for a child who is less than 18 or disabled and entitled to benefits	Fully or currently insured
Dependent child	Fully or currently insured
Widower 60 or older, or disabled widower, 50 or older	Fully insured
Dependent parent 62 or older	Fully insured
Lump-sum death payment	Fully or currently insured
You and your dependents if you are disabled	Fully insured and meet work requirements

Question: My problem may be unusual. The maximum wage that Social Security contributions could be taken from in 1980 was $25,900. Well, in three months I earned a little over $27,000 and for the rest of the year I didn't do a stitch of work. Am I going to be credited for only a quarter-year of work, even though I went over the maximum?

Answer: No. Any employee who earns the maximum in a year, even if it took him only part of the year to do it, gets a full year of work credit. Naturally, this does not mean you

HAVE to stop working once you reach the maximum. And the maximum for 1981 is $29,700. Similarly, you don't have to work the entire three months of a calendar quarter to get credit for a quarter-year of work. As long as you earn at least $310 during the three months, you get credit for the entire quarter, even if you were able to earn the $310 in a day or an hour.

Question: I want to get work credit so I, too, can draw Social Security benefits later on. But I really can't leave the house because I have small children. Is there any kind of work I could do at home that would give me credit under Social Security?

Answer: Yes. Some examples are writing, selling merchandise (such as candy, greeting cards or magazines) by mail or by telephone, typing (a number of college students pay outsiders to type their term papers and other assignments), teaching (whether it's one piano student or a roomful of needlepoint amateurs), sewing, repairing dolls, and so on. Because the work requirements depend on whether your new job is considered self-employment or employee-employer employment, you should contact your Social Security office. The staff there can advise you and also tell you how much you must earn each quarter to get Social Security coverage.

Question: What if I stop working before I've earned enough credit to be insured?

Answer: You will not be eligible for benefits. However, the credit you do have will remain on your records, just in case you decide to go back to work.

Question: I'm already receiving retirement benefits, but have decided to go back to work. How will this affect my benefits?

Answer: You will never have more than $1 in benefits withheld for each $2 you earn—and you can earn up to $5,500 if you are 65 or over or $4,080 if you are under 65 in a year with no benefits withheld. Thus, the more you earn, the higher your total income—earnings plus Social Security benefits—will be.

Question: If I go back to work after starting to collect retirement benefits, will my earnings affect the benefits that my dependents get?

Answer: They may. Your Social Security office will tell you. However, if you get benefits as a dependent or survivor, your earnings will affect only your benefits, not the benefits of others in your family.

Question: If I'm eligible for benefits, will they be given to me automatically?

Answer: No. You must apply for them.

Question: How do I apply for benefits?

Answer: When you are approaching the age of 65 (62 if you are interested in early, but reduced, benefits), or when you become disabled, contact your Social Security office. Even if you don't plan to retire, you should contact the office two or three months before your 65th (or 62nd) birthday. Your benefit amount may need to be refigured upward on the basis of high earnings you made in the year you became 65 (or 62) or later. Too, you will lose at least one month of Medicare protection if you wait until the month you became 65 before applying for the medical-insurance part of Medicare.

Question: I want to make sure my family doesn't lose any of my benefits when I die. What should they do when I pass away?

Answer: Some member of your family should contact your Social Security office. If it is impossible to stop in, a Social Security representative can arrange to visit your family.

Question: What if something happens and I can't get away from home to apply for benefits at the Social Security office?

Answer: The office can take your application over the telephone.

Question: I just never got around to applying for my Social Security benefits. Will I lose anything because of the delay?

Answer: Possibly. There are situations in which there are

no back benefits payable. And an application for a lump-sum death payment usually must be made within two years of the worker's death.

Question: Will I have to bring any papers or anything with me when I apply for my benefits?

Answer: Yes. Take your Social Security card, or at least the number; proof of your age, such as a birth certificate made at or shortly after your birth; and your Wage and Tax Statement (the W-2 form) for the previous year (unless you are self-employed, in which case take a copy of your last Federal income tax return).

If your application is based on the earnings of another person, take that person's Social Security card or Social Security number. If you are applying for a wife's, husband's, widow's or widower's benefits, take his or her birth certificate. If your children are eligible for benefits, take their birth certificates. If your working son or daughter has died, you must show proof that you were being supported by the insured person if you want to receive benefits. The proof generally must be supplied within two years after the insured worker dies or applies for benefits.

Question: What if I can't furnish all the necessary papers?

Answer: Apply anyway. The staff at your Social Security office can tell you about alternative ways of proving your claim. In your application, state why you do not have the necessary documents.

Question: Can creditors seize my benefits if I go into debt?

Answer: No.

Question: Someone stole my benefit check. What should I do?

Answer: Contact your Social Security office. The check will be replaced.

Question: I somehow lost my benefit check. Can anything be done?

Answer: Contact your Social Security office. The check will be replaced. Do the same if your check arrives damaged.

Question: I'm so afraid that my check will be stolen before it gets to me, or that I'll lose it once it gets here. Is there a safer way to get my checks?

Answer: You can ask your Social Security office to mail your checks to you in care of your bank or savings and loan association, where it can be deposited automatically in your savings or checking account. There is no charge for this arrangement. The form that you need is available at your bank.

Question: My husband and I are going to take a four-month vacation abroad as a retirement present to ourselves. Can we arrange for our retirement checks to be sent to a bank outside the United States? We don't want them accumulating at the post office and we won't be staying very long in one place during our vacation.

Answer: If your bank agrees (phone them), this can be done. You will have to fill out and give to your bank a power-of-attorney form (Treasury Standard From 233), which is valid for one year. Give your bank's address to your Social Security office. Then bon voyage. If you decide to take a longer trip next year—six months or more—other rules will apply and you should again contact your Social Security office.

Question: I'm moving. How do I report my new address?

Answer: Call your Social Security office, and remember to include your zip code. If you don't know your zip code, call your post office first.

Question: Will I lose any benefits or have to reapply for them if I move to another city?

Answer: No. Nor if you move to another state. Just remember to give your new address to your Social Security office.

Question: I'm not receiving any benefits as yet (I'm only 24), just amassing as much work credits as I can. Do I have to give notice to Social Security if I move from job to job or from city to city or from state to state?

Answer: No. Every employer you have will be getting the same Social Security number from you and will be forwarding your Social Security contributions to the same Social Security Administration. So all your work credits will work their way to your permanent records in Baltimore.

Question: I applied for retirement benefits three months before I retired, just as Social Security suggested, and had all the required documents with me. That was six weeks ago, and still no benefits. What can I do?

Answer: Contact your Social Security office. There are special procedures for getting payments started when there are delays like yours.

Question: My application for Social Security benefits was denied, but I don't think it should have been. What recourse do I have?

Answer: You can appeal the decision, without cost, by signing a "Request for Reconsideration" form at any Social Security office. If you are still not satisfied with the result, you can request a hearing before an independent hearing officer at your local Bureau of Hearings and Appeals, which is part of the U.S. Department of Health and Human Services. If the hearing officer rules against you, you can appeal the ruling, again without cost, to the Hearings and Appeals office in Washington, D.C.

RETIREMENT BENEFITS

While the concept of Social Security has grown from a modest pension to encompass many areas of social welfare today, it's primary goal is still to provide a basic retirement income for people who, after a lifetime of work, are no longer gainfully employed.

The need for retirement income is universal. Young and middle-aged workers are ordinarily willing to pay for Social Security benefits and private pensions. It is not really a question of younger workers doing something for retired people. No one remains young forever and current workers and retirees have a common interest in making certain that Social Security and other arrangements for retirement income are adequate and built on a sound foundation.

Of course, most people don't *want* to retire. A recent survey showed that among newly entitled beneficiaries of retirement age, 65 per cent did not want to retire but retired at their employer's initiative or because of ill health. Of people who reached compulsory retirement age in government jobs and in companies that have such rulings, 52 per cent of the men and 58 per cent of the women said they did not want to retire.

One problem is that the opportunity to work is greatly restricted in old age. Companies feel it is uneconomical to hire older workers on a full-time basis, and ill health keeps many workers from continuing to earn money in old age.

WHEN CAN I RETIRE?

Social Security retirement benefits can be paid as early as age 62. But, if your benefits start before 65, the amount of your checks will be reduced to take account of the longer period you will be getting them.

The amount of the reduction depends on the number of months you receive benefits before you become 65. The reduction amounts to 20 percent at 62; 13⅓ per cent at 63; and 6⅔ per cent at 64.

WHO GETS BENEFITS?

When you retire, checks can be paid to certain members of your family. Monthly checks can go to your unmarried children under 18, or 22 if full-time students, or 18 or over who were severely disabled before 22 and who continue to be disabled; your wife or husband 62 or over; and your wife under 62 if she's caring for your child under 18 (or disabled) who's getting checks on your record.

WHEN TO APPLY

If you haven't applied before, be sure to apply two or three months before you reach 65 so that you will have full Medicare protection the month you reach 65. If you wait until the month you are 65 or later, your Medicare health insurance coverage will be delayed at least one month.

This is important because many commercial and non-profit health insurance plans adjust their coverage when a person reaches 65 to take account of Medicare coverage. You may want to get in touch with your insurance agent or the office where you pay health insurance premiums to discuss your health insurance needs in relation to Medicare protection. This is particularly important if you have dependents who are covered under your present policy. But do not cancel any health insurance you have until the month your Medicare coverage begins.

Once you decide when you will retire, apply for your Social Security retirement checks two or three months before you plan to stop working. This way, your benefits will start when your income from work stops.

If you work past 65, your monthly benefit will be increased by 1 per cent for each year ($\frac{1}{12}$ per cent for each month) that you don't get a benefit because of your work. For people who reach 65 in 1982 or later, the credit will be 3 per cent for each year ($\frac{1}{4}$ per cent for each month).

HOW TO APPLY FOR RETIREMENT BENEFITS

There are two ways to apply and you can do it either way. You can apply in person or you can do it over the telephone. Many people find it more convenient to use the phone so they don't have to travel to the office.

Once you've been interviewed by phone, the rest can be done by mail.

DOCUMENTS YOU WILL NEED

You need your Social Security card, or a record of the number.

Next, you need proof of your date of birth. You should submit an official record of your birth or baptism recorded early in life. If this is not possible, submit the best evidence you have available. The best is often the oldest. If you're not sure what is best, call any Social Security office. They can tell you what kind of documents are acceptable.

Other records that might be acceptable include school, church, state or Federal census, insurance policies, marriage, passports, employment, military service, children's birth certificates, union, immigration, and naturalization. This is not an exclusive list and there are other records which may prove acceptable.

Take your W-2 (Wage and Tax Statement) forms for the last two years, or, if you're self-employed, copies of self-employment tax returns for the last two years.

If your husband or wife is also going to apply for benefits, he or she will need pretty much the same documents. It would also be a good idea to have your marriage certificate available, although this is not always needed. If either of you were married before, they will need information about the duration of the previous marriages.

If you have eligible unmarried children, you should take along their birth certificates, together with a record of the Social Security numbers if available.

WHEN DO CHECKS START?

If you apply two or three months before your retirement month, your checks should start the month you retire. If you apply closer to that month or after, your checks will start six to eight weeks after you apply and Social Security has all the required supporting evidence.

WHAT ABOUT RETURNING TO WORK?

You can work after you become eligible for Social Security checks. The question is: how much can you earn and still get checks? The answer to this question depends on your age.

Over 65

If you are 65 or older in 1981, you can earn $5,500 this year and receive all benefits due you for the year. This annual exempt amount will increase to $6,000 for 1982. After that, it will increase automatically to keep pace with increases in average covered wages.

Under 65

If you are under 65 in 1981, you can earn $4,080 this year and receive all benefits due you for the year. This annual exempt amount will increase automatically in future years to keep pace with increases in annual covered wages.

If your earnings exceed the annual exempt amount, $1 in benefits will be withheld for each $2 of earnings above the exempt amount.

There is a special rule that applies to people only in the year they retire. Under this rule, even though earnings exceed the annual exempt amount, a benefit can be paid for any month the person's wages do not exceed the monthly limit and the person does not perform substantial services in self-employment. The 1981 monthly limit is $459 for people 65 or over and $340 for people under 65.

HOW MUCH DO I GET?

Your benefit rate depends on the amount of earnings reported for you. The higher your earnings over the years, the higher your benefit rate will be.

Right now, benefits payable to a retired worker who reaches 65 this year range from $153.10 to $677 a month. The range for a worker who reaches 62 this year is from $111.50 to 460.40 a month.

If you have eligible dependents and you are 65, the range for a family is from $229.70 to $1,184.70 a month. If you're 62 this year, the range is from $181.70 to $892 a month.

Once you are on the Social Security benefit rolls, your checks will increase automatically to keep pace with increases in the cost of living. Each year, living costs are compared to those of the previous year. If the cost of living has increased by three per cent or more from one year to the next, benefit rates will be increased by the same percentage the following July.

Benefits for 1981-1982, tied to the cost of living, were increased by 11.2 per cent, and the increase is first shown in the check for July 1981.

In order to get a rough idea of the benefits you might collect, see the following chart:

Monthly retirement benefits for workers who reached 62 before 1979
(effective June 1980)

	For Workers			For Dependents[1]				
Average yearly earnings	Retirement at 65	at 64	at 63	Spouse at 65 or child	at 64	at 63	at 62	Family[2] benefits
$923 or less	153.10	142.90	132.70	76.60	70.30	63.90	57.50	229.70
1,200	197.00	183.90	170.80	98.50	90.30	82.10	73.90	295.50
2,000	256.20	239.20	222.10	128.10	117.50	106.80	96.10	384.30
3,000	316.40	295.40	274.30	158.20	145.10	131.90	118.70	483.70
3,600	349.50	326.20	302.90	174.80	160.30	145.70	131.10	573.00
4,000	372.20	347.40	322.60	186.10	170.60	155.10	139.60	636.00
4,400	398.70	372.20	345.60	199.40	182.80	166.20	149.60	706.70
4,800	422.20	394.10	366.00	211.10	193.60	176.00	158.40	769.70
5,200	443.80	414.30	384.70	221.90	203.50	185.00	166.50	832.60
5,600	465.60	434.60	403.60	232.80	213.00	193.60	174.30	863.20
6,000	487.80	455.30	422.80	243.90	223.60	203.30	183.00	894.60
6,400	509.60	475.70	441.70	254.80	233.60	212.40	191.10	926.00
6,800	532.80	497.30	461.80	266.40	244.20	222.00	199.80	957.70
7,200	560.30	523.00	485.60	280.20	256.90	233.50	210.20	991.10
7,600	584.90	546.00	507.00	292.50	268.20	243.80	219.40	1,023.50
8,000	606.30	565.90	525.50	303.20	278.00	252.70	227.40	1,061.00
8,400	619.20	578.00	536.70	309.60	283.80	258.00	232.20	1,083.60
8,800	634.60	592.30	550.00	317.30	290.90	264.50	238.00	1,110.20
9,400	653.80	610.30	566.70	326.90	299.70	272.50	245.20	1,143.70
10,000	671.80	627.10	582.30	335.90	308.00	280.00	252.00	1,175.50
10,400	684.50	638.90	593.30	342.30	313.80	285.30	256.80	1,197.50
11,000	702.70	655.90	609.10	351.40	322.20	292.90	263.60	1,229.00
11,400	713.30	665.80	618.20	356.70	327.00	297.30	267.60	1,248.10

[1] If a person is eligible for both a worker's benefit and a spouse's benefit, the check actually payable is limited to the larger of the two.

[2] The maximum amount payable to a family is generally reached when a worker and two family members are eligible.

WILL YOU GET MAXIMUM BENEFITS?

Some people think that if they've always earned the maximum amount covered by Social Security they will get the highest benefits shown on the chart. This isn't so. For people reaching 65 in 1980, the maximum monthly benefit is $653.80. The reason is that the maximum amount of earnings covered by Social Security was lower in past years than it is now. Those years of lower limits must be counted in with the higher ones of recent years to figure your *average* earnings and thus the amount of your monthly retirement check.

QUESTIONS AND ANSWERS

Question: How will the size of my retirement benefits be determined?

Answer: All your earnings for work covered by Social Security will be averaged, either from 1937 on or from 1951 on, and your benefits will be based on whichever figure is higher. Generally, using your earnings from 1951 on will give you higher benefits because wages have increased so much since 1951. The lower wages paid in the 1937-1951 period might draw down your average. The staff at your Social Security office will help you decide which years to use when you apply for retirement benefits.

Question: I'd like to get an idea now of how much I'll be getting. Is it possible to do so?

Answer: Yes. If you are 61 years old or older, your Social Security office can give you an estimate of how much you would collect if you retired at age 62, 63, 64 and 65. Thus the estimate will show you not only how much you can expect to get at age 65, but also how much your benefits would be reduced if you retire earlier.

Question: I'm 65 but I'd rather work than retire, and that's what I'm going to do. How will this affect my benefits later on, when I do decide to retire?

Answer: The amount will increase because your additional earnings will be credited on your records. And regardless of whether you choose to keep on working, for workers reaching 65 after 1981, if you delay your retirement past age 65 you will get an increase in retirement benefits of 3 per cent per year—1/4 of 1 per cent for each month—for each year between age 65 and 72 that you do not get benefits. However, you must have earnings after December 31, 1970, to qualify.

Your dependents who became eligible before December 1978 to a reduced benefit may have his/her benefit increased by 1/2 of 1 per cent for each month, effective January 1979 or later.

Question: My wages were so low during my working years that I'm afraid my benefits aren't going to amount to much when I become eligible for them. Will I be forced to get by on skimpy benefits?

Answer: There is a special minimum retirement benefit for people who worked under Social Security for more than 20 years—a provision that could aid people like you whose incomes during working years were low. The size of the payment depends on the number of years you worked. For example, if you retire at age 65 with 30 years of work under Social Security, the special minimum is $289. The payment drops $9 for each year under 30 payable years before 1979 and by $11.50 for benefits payable for 1979 and later. Most people who have worked 20 years or more under Social Security already get benefits higher than the special minimum.

Question: If I decide to go back to work after I start getting retirement benefits, will my benefits be reduced because of the extra income I'll be getting?

Answer: If you are 65 years old or older, you can earn up to $5,500; under 65 years of age, you can earn up to $4,080 with no loss in benefits.

Question: I know that additional earnings may affect the size of my benefits. But what about things like interest on my savings accounts and capital gains on my investment? Will these be figured against my benefits?

Answer: No. Nor will insurance endowments, income from private or veterans' pensions, stocks and bonds, annuities, gifts, inheritances, income from retirement programs, rental income from property (unless you are a real-estate dealer and the property is part of your business), royalties received in or after the year in which you reach 65 on patents or copyrights established before the taxable year in which you reach 65. If you are a farmer and are renting out your farm, your Social Security office can tell you whether your benefits will be affected.

Question: When I start getting my retirement benefits, can my wife (or husband) and children get benefits also?

Answer: Your wife or husband will be eligible if she (or he) is 62 years old or older, or if she is caring for an unmarried child less than 18 years old or a disabled child less than 22. Such children as well as any children less than 22 years old who are still going to school also are eligible.

Question: How much can my wife and children get?

Answer: If your wife is at least 65 years old she can collect an amount equal to 50 percent of what you would get if you began collecting at age 65. Each of your children would collect the same. If your wife wants to collect before she is 65 years old (but after she is 62), her payments will be reduced, unless she is caring for a child.

Question: If each of my kids can collect half of what I collect, then if I had 20 kids I'd really be living in style, wouldn't I?

Answer: There is a limit on the amount of benefits one family can collect. In June, 1980, the limits ranged from $229.70 to $967.90, depending on how much the worker himself was eligible for. And not many people of retirement age have 20 children less than 22 years old. But it still is possible to live in style.

Question: My husband and I were divorced three years ago. He has since retired. Can I collect benefits based on his earnings?

Answer: Yes, if you are 62 years old or older and were married to your former husband for at least 10 years.

Question: My ex-husband retired five years ago and I've been collecting the benefits due me. But he plans to remarry this fall. Will I lose the benefits?

RETIREMENT BENEFITS

Answer: No. You will collect full benefits on the same basis as would a dependent wife. This applies to other former wives your husband may have.

Question: I've been collecting benefits based on my ex-husband's work record ever since he retired. Now I'm planning to remarry (not him, another man). Will I lose the benefits I get from my ex-husband?

Answer: Generally, yes. But if you are 62 years old or older you can keep collecting benefits by marrying a man who is also collecting. You can then choose to collect on the basis of whichever husband had the higher earnings.

Question: We've worked all our lives in the U.S.A., but we plan to retire abroad. Can our benefits be paid to us outside the United States.

Answer: Yes, although there are special rules. If you plan to be outside the country for 30 days or more while you are collecting benefits, contact your Social Security office and ask for the SSA-10137 leaflet. There are also special rules if you are not a citizen or a national of the United States.

Question: I've reached retirement age at last, but haven't been living with my husband for several months. Can I still draw my benefits based on his work record?

Answer: Yes, but only if your husband starts collecting his benefits at age 62 or later. In addition, if you are 65 years old and your husband is at least 62, you can get Medicare on his record, if he agrees to apply.

Question: Even though I'm a man, I've been supporting women's rights right along. My wife has done most of the working and has provided most of my support. Now she's retired and I'm wondering—can I get benefits based on her earnings records?

Answer: Yes, if you are 62 years old or older.

Question: I never got to work when my husband and I were younger because someone had to stay home and take care of the house and the children. So when my husband retired, I had my chance. Now I go to work and he takes care of the house (our children are grown and have to take care of themselves). But will my earnings affect my husband's benefits?

Answer: No. But if you earn more than $5,500 if you are 65 or older or $4,080 if you are under 65 in a year after you yourself retire, your benefits will be reduced (unless you are 72 years old or older, in which case you can earn as much as you want with no benefit reductions).

Question: Are grandchildren entitled to benefits based on a worker's earnings record?

Answer: Yes, if the grandchild's natural or adoptive parents are disabled or dead, and if the child was living with the worker and was receiving at least half of his support from that worker during the year before the worker became disabled, became eligible for retirement or disability benefits, or died. The child may also be eligible if he began living with the worker before he reached age 18.

DISABILITY BENEFITS

Social Security is a disability insurance policy as well as a retirement plan. There is extensive protection available for disabled workers and their dependents and more than three million people today are benefiting from this protection.

You become eligible for disability benefits if you are a worker or the dependent of a worker who has been stricken by a disease or an injury or mental condition that will keep you out of work for a minimum of a year, or that could be the cause of death.

If you meet these conditions, you may be able to get payments even if your recovery from the disability is expected.

The medical evidence from your physician or other sources will show the severity of your condition and the extent which it prevents you from being gainfully employed. Your age, education, training, and work experience also may be considered in deciding whether you are able to work.

If you can't do your regular work but can do other substantial gainful work, you will probably not be considered disabled.

SEPARATE REQUIREMENTS FOR THE BLIND

A person whose vision is no better than 20/200 even with glasses, or who has a limited visual field of 20 degrees or less, is considered "blind" under the Social Security law.

If you meet this test of blindness and have worked long enough under Social Security, you are eligible for a disability "freeze" even if you are actually working. This means that your future benefits, which are figured from your average earnings, will not be reduced because you have low earnings or no earnings in those years in which you were disabled.

If you are 55 to 65, meet this test of blindness, and have worked long enough under Social Security, you may get cash disability benefits if you are unable to perform work requiring skills or abilities comparable to those required by the work you did regularly before you reached 55 or became blind, whichever is later. Benefits will not be paid, however, for any month in which you *actually* perform substantial gainful work.

People disabled because of blindness have a special measure of "substantial gainful activity." A person getting benefits because of blindness is considered to be engaging in substantial gainful activity if his or her earnings exceed $417 a month in 1980. The monthly measure will be higher in future years.

WORK CREDITS FOR DISABILITY BENEFITS

As with retirement benefits, you must have accumulated a number of work credits before you can be eligible for disability benefits. If you are under 24 years of age, you must be fully insured and have accumulated six work credits during the three years before you became disabled. Since you can earn a maximum of four work credits in any calendar year, the requirement is to have worked for at least one-and-a-half years during the past three.

If you are between 24 and 30, you must have earned two work credits for each year after you turned 21, or you must have worked at least half the time. Over 31, the requirement continues to be half of the working time. You must have earned 20 work credits during the 40 quarters before you were disabled.

As with retirement benefits, in order to collect any payments for disability, you must have earned the minimum number of work credits.

FILING FOR DISABILITY BENEFITS

As soon as you find out that a current illness or injury may keep you out of work for a year or more, you should contact your Social Security office. Taking care of your application is a stringent process that involves consultation with medical experts and career counselors. Then, if you have the required work credits and your claim is accepted, by law you must wait five months from the time of your disability for your first benefit check. This waiting period allows time for a further evaluation of your condition.

Judgment on whether your condition qualifies you for benefits is made by a state agency. But this does not have to be the final word. If you are turned down for benefits, you can ask to have your case reconsidered within 60 days. If you want your case reconsidered, however, you should be able to bring additional information to the attention of the agency. If you are once again denied benefits, you can still get a hearing on your case before an administrative judge. Often, initial denials are reversed and all payments are retroactive to the time of your disability plus the five-month waiting period.

While it is best to file as soon as you can for disability benefits, there is no time limit for filing. You may even file for past benefits after a number of years have passed. But if you apply and are awarded benefits for a past disability, you can collect only a maximum of 12 months back benefits.

RECEIVING DISABILITY BENEFITS WHILE WORKING

If you are receiving disability benefits and you want to return to work, though you are not sure of your capacity, Social Security will often permit you to return to work for a trial period while you are still collecting disability benefits. The trial period is nine months which are not necessarily consecutive, but can consist of a month or two and then another period of time, until the total comes to nine months.

During this period you can earn as much as possible while continuing to collect full disability payments.

HOW MUCH AND HOW LONG

The amount of any disability payment depends on the same factors that govern retirement benefits. Primarily it depends on how much you earned under Social Security and for how long. As far as how long you may collect disability benefits, payments are made for the length of the disability, plus an extra two months *after* the disability has ended and you have returned to work.

DEPENDENTS AND DISABILITY

Social Security pays benefits to dependents of a disabled worker in the same way as if you had retired. Your husband or wife and children each get half of your entitlement up to the family maximum until your children turn 18 or marry, when spouse's benefits are terminated. Your children, though, can keep on receiving benefits until they are 22 as long as they stay in school. If you have no children under the maximum age, neither they nor your spouse may collect any benefits. If your spouse is 62 or more, he or she can collect benefits as if you had retired.

Survivors of a disabled worker who has died may also be eligible for disability benefits. If the worker did not apply for benefits, the survivors may file for him during the three months after his death. Any benefits due will be paid to the survivors retroactively. A disabled survivor of a deceased worker can also be eligible for disability benefits. If you are between 50 and 60 years old and are a disabled widow or widower, you can receive reduced widow or widower's benefits.

DISABLED BEFORE AGE 22

If you have an unmarried son or daughter 18 or older who became disabled before 22 and is still disabled, he or she may start receiving disability benefits when you start getting Social Security retirement or disability benefits, or at your death if you had enough Social Security work credits for the payment of benefits to your survivors.

A person disabled before 22 needs no Social Security work credits to get benefits. The payments, based on the earnings of a parent, may continue for as long as he or she is disabled and the parent's eligibility continues. The decision whether a person has been disabled since childhood is made in the same way as the decision whether a worker is disabled.

If a child with a severe medical condition is now receiving child's benefits which are scheduled to stop at age 18, the child or someone in the family should get in touch with the Social Security office a few months before the 18th birthday to see about continuing the benefits past 18 on the basis of disability.

If a disability first occurs between the ages of 18 and 22, an application should be filed at that time or later when benefits are payable on the Social Security work record of a parent.

The mother of a disabled son or daughter who is entitled to disability benefits may also qualify for benefits *regardless of her age* if she has the son or daughter in her care.

DISABLED WIDOWS OR WIDOWERS

If you are disabled and are the widow, widower or, under certain circumstances, the surviving divorced wife of a worker who worked long enough under Social Security, you may be able to get monthly benefits as early as age 50. The benefits will be permanently reduced, with the amount of the reduction depending on the age when benefits start. You need no work credits of your own to get benefits based on the earnings of a deceased spouse.

A widow or widower may be considered disabled only if she or he has an impairment which is so severe that it would ordinarily prevent a person from working and is expected to last at least 12 months. Vocational factors such as age, education, and previous work experience cannot be considered in deciding whether a widow or widower is disabled as they may be for a disabled worker.

In general, you cannot get these benefits unless your disability starts before your spouse's death or within seven years after the death. However, if you receive benefits as a widow with children, you can be eligible if you become disabled before those payments end or within seven years after they end. This seven-year period allows the widow a chance to earn enough work credits for disability protection on her own Social Security record.

A disabled surviving divorced wife may get benefits based on the earnings of her former husband only if their marriage lasted ten years or longer.

DISABILITY BENEFITS AND WORKMEN'S COMPENSATIONS

Workmen's Compensation benefits are ordered by law in most states. These laws require that medical care and monetary aid be awarded to workmen who are injured on the job and that survivor's benefits be awarded to dependents of workers who are killed in job-related ways.

You can collect *both* Workmen's Compensation and Social Security disability benefits, although disability benefits may be reduced. You may collect a combination of Social Security disability and Workman's Compensation up to 80 per cent of your average current earnings. If, for example, your average wages were $1,000 a month and you were collecting $350 a month from Workmen's Compensation and Social Security benefits of $550 a month, you would be receiving $900 a month, or 90 per cent of your average wage. In this case, the Social Security disability payment would be reduced to bring total payments in line with the 80 per cent requirement and your disability payment would be $450 a month.

If you are collecting Workmen's Compensation payments and have reached retirement age and apply for Social Security retirement benefits, you may receive both payments simultaneously. In this case, your Social Security benefit will be unaffected by the amount of Workmen's Compensation you receive, since Workmen's Compensation is considered unearned income and retirement benefits are not altered by unearned income.

MEDICARE FOR THE DISABLED

Certain disabled people under 65 are eligible for Medicare. They include disabled workers at any age, persons who became disabled before age 22, and disabled widows and widowers age 50 or over who have been entitled to disability checks for two years or more.

Medicare protection generally ends when monthly disability benefits end. But after December 1980, Medicare continues an additional three years after benefits stop because an individual returns to gainful work.

Also after December 1980, if a person becomes entitled to disability benefits again, Medicare coverage starts at the same time if a worker becomes disabled again within five years after benefits end, or within seven years for a disabled widow, widower, or person disabled before age 22.

Medicare for Those with Permanent Kidney Failure

Those who need long-term dialysis treatment or a kidney transplant for permanent kidney failure can be covered by Medicare. People who have worked long enough under Social Security to be insured, people getting monthly benefits, and the wives or husbands and dependent children of insured people and beneficiaries will be eligible if they need maintenance dialysis or a kidney transplant.

AMOUNT OF BENEFITS

Benefits to workers disabled after 1978 and their dependents are based, in part, on earnings that have been adjusted to take account of increases in average wages since they were earned. The adjusted earnings are averaged together and a formula is applied to the adjusted average to figure the benefit rate.

Monthly benefits in July 1980 or later range from $139.50 to $647 for a worker and go as high as $970.50 for a worker with a family. Once a person starts receiving benefits, the amount will increase automatically in future years to keep pace with the rising cost of living.

DISABILITY AND OTHER SOCIAL SECURITY BENEFITS

Benefits because of disability are not paid in addition to other monthly Social Security benefits. If you become entitled to more than one monthly benefit at the same time, the amount you receive will ordinarily be equal to the larger of the benefits.

If you become disabled after you start receiving Social Security benefits, it may be to your advantage to switch over to benefits based on disability. For instance, if you start receiving reduced retirement benefits at 62 and then become disabled at 63, your benefit may be higher if you change to disability payments.

HOW WORK AFFECTS BENEFITS

If you receive benefits as a disabled worker, an adult disabled since childhood, or a disabled widow or widower, you are not subject to the general rule under which some benefits are withheld if you have substantial earnings. There are special rules, which include medical considerations, for determining how any work you do might affect your disability payments.

If one of your dependents who is under 65 and who is not disabled works and earns more than $4,080 in 1981, some of the dependent's benefits may be withheld. In general, $1 in benefits is withheld for each $2 over $4,080.

Different rules apply to your dependents who are 65 or over.

The amount a person can earn without having any benefits withheld will increase in future years as the level of average wages rises.

WHAT ARE DISABLING CONDITIONS?

Conditions which are severe enough to be considered disabling under the law are fully described in the Social Security Regulations. A brief example of some of those conditions includes:

1. Loss of major function of both arms, both legs, or a leg and an arm.

2. Progressive diseases which have resulted in the loss of a leg or which have caused it to become useless.

3. Severe arthritis which causes recurrent inflammation, pain, swelling, and deformity in major joints so that the ability to get about or use the hands has been severely limited.

4. Diseases of heart, lung, or blood vessels which have resulted in serious loss of heart or lung reserve as shown by X-ray, electro-

cardiogram, or other tests; and, in spite of medical treatment, there is breathlessness, pain, or fatigue.

5. Diseases of the digestive system which result in severe malnutrition, weakness, and anemia.

6. Serious loss of function of the kidneys.

7. Cancer which is progressive and has not been controlled or cured.

8. Damage to the brain or brain abnormality which has resulted in severe loss of judgment, intellect, orientation, or memory.

9. Mental illness resulting in marked constriction of activities and interests, deterioration in personal habits, and seriously impaired ability to get along with other people.

10. Total inability to speak.

In the case of workers and people disabled before 22, conditions less severe than those listed in the Regulations can be considered disabling. This is because age, education, training, and work experience can also be taken into account for these applicants.

VOCATIONAL REHABILITATION AND EMPLOYMENT SERVICES

Whether or not you are found eligible to receive benefits because of disability, you may be offered help in improving your condition and in preparing for and finding work.

When you apply for Social Security disability benefits, you will be considered for vocational rehabilitation services by your state vocational rehabilitation agency. That agency provides counseling, training, and other services that you may need to help you get back to work. Information in your file is made available to help the people in that agency decide whether you can benefit from rehabilitation services and, if so, what kinds of services will be most useful to you.

Rehabilitation services generally are financed by state-Federal funds. In some cases, however, Social Security pays the costs of rehabilitating those receiving disability benefits. Rehabilitating beneficiaries is expected to save Social Security money because, in the long run, the cost should be less than the expense of paying them benefits.

You may also get employment counseling and special placement services from your State Employment Service.

People who become entitled to benefits because of disability will not be paid those benefits if, without good cause, they refuse counseling, training, or other services offered to them by their state vocational rehabilitation agencies.

QUESTIONS AND ANSWERS

Question: Who can collect disability benefits?

Answer: The benefits can be paid to disabled workers less than 65 years old and their families, to people disabled before age 22 who continue to be disabled, to disabled widows, to disabled widowers and, under certain conditions, to disabled surviving divorced wives of workers who were insured at death.

Question: Can all members of my family get payments if I'm receiving disability benefits?

Answer: Payments can be made to unmarried children under age 18, to unmarried children age 18 through 21 who are attending school full time, to unmarried children 18 years old or older who were disabled before age 22 and continue to be disabled, to stepchildren, to adopted children, to a wife at any age if she is caring for a child who is getting benefits because he is under age 18, or has been disabled since before age 18; to a wife 62 years old or older, and to a husband age 62 or older.

Question: How soon can benefits be paid to a child disabled before age 22 who remains disabled?

Answer: Benefits can be paid as early as age 18 if a parent (or a grandparent under certain conditions) receives Social Security retirement or disability benefits or if an insured parent dies.

Question: How does the Social Security Administration define "disabled?"

Answer: A worker is considered disabled if a physical or mental impairment prevents him from doing any substantial gainful work and is expected to last (or has lasted) at least 12 months, or is expected to result in death. Other government programs or private disability insurance programs may use a different definition, so meeting the disability test of other programs doesn't guarantee that you'll be eligible for Social Security disability payments.

Question: Could you give some examples of impairments that Social Security would consider disabling?

Answer: Some examples are total inability to speak; loss of major function of both arms, both legs or a leg and an arm; mental illness that results in a marked constriction of activities and interests, a deterioration in personal habits and seriously impaired ability to get along with other people; progressive diseases that result in the loss of a leg, or that have made a leg useless; brain damage or a brain abnormality resulting in a severe loss of judgment, intellect, orientation or memory; severe arthritis that seriously limits the ability to get about or to use the hands; progressive cancer that has not been controlled or cured; diseases of the heart, lungs, or blood vessels that have seriously damaged the heart or lungs as shown by tests; serious kidney damage, and diseases of the digestive system that result in severe malnutrition, weakness and anemia.

Question: I was disabled in childhood, but my condition isn't as severe as the ones you listed. Does that mean I'm really not considered disabled?

Answer: No. For workers and people disabled since childhood, less severe conditions may be considered disabling because education, training and work experience, which may have been less accessible to you, will be taken into account in such cases.

Question: Does my disability have to be permanent if I'm to get disability payments?

Answer: No. But it must be expected to last at least 12 months (or result in death).

Question: Do I need any work credits to get disability benefits?

DISABILITY BENEFITS

Answer: Yes. If you become disabled before age 24, you will need credit for one and a half years of work in the three years before you become disabled. If you become disabled when you are 24 through 30 years old, you will need work credit for half of the time between age 21 and the time you become disabled. If you become disabled at age 31 or older (unless you are blind), you will need credit for at least five years of work during the 10 years before you become disabled. Some workers, however, may need more credits, depending on their age and time of disability.

Question: How much work credit does a blind person need?

Answer: You need credit for one-quarter year of work for each year since 1950, or since the year you became 21 if you became 21 after 1950, up to the year you became blind. The credit must total at least one and a half years.

Question: Let's say I become disabled when I'm 37. That means I'll need five years of work credit for the preceding 10 years. Does it have to be five years in a row, or can it be a full year here, half a year there, two years there, as long as it adds up to five years?

Answer: The work does not have to be continuous or in units of full years. This is true whether you become disabled after age 31 and need five years of work credit, or whether you become disabled when you are younger and need fewer years of credit.

Question: What will determine the size of my disability benefits?

Answer: The amount of your payment, as well as the amount of the payments to your dependents, will depend on the amount of your average earnings under Social Security over a period of years.

Question: Can I find out in advance how much I would collect if I became disabled?

Answer: You can't find out the exact amount because all of your covered earnings right up to the time of your application would have to be considered. But there is a formula you can use now to get an estimate. (The formula works only if you have at least two years of earnings.)

Step 1. If you were born before Jan. 1, 1930, subtract the year 1956 from the year you became disabled. If you were born after Dec. 31, 1929, subtract the year in which you became 27 years old from the year you became disabled. This will give you the number of years to be used in figuring your average earnings.

Step 2. Write down your earnings for all years starting with 1951, including the year you become disabled. However, do not list more than $3,600 for each year 1951 through 1954; $4,200 for each year 1955 through 1958; $4,800 for each year 1959 through 1965; $6,600 for 1966 and 1967; $7,800 for each year 1968 through 1971; $9,000 for 1972; $10,800 for 1973; $13,200 for 1974; $14,100 for 1975; $15,300 for 1976; $16,500 1977; $17,700 for 1978; $22,900 for 1979; and $25,900 for 1980.

Step 3. Cross off the years with the lowest earnings until the number of years remaining is the same as your
Step answer to Step 1. You may have to leave in years in which you had no earnings.

Step 4. Add up the earnings for the years left on your list, and divide the total earnings by the number of years used (your answer to Step 1). Then use the table on p. 57 to estimate your benefits.

Question: I notice that the first figure in the top line of the table is "$923 or less." My earnings haven't amounted to much. How much less than $923 can I go and still get the $153.10 in disability benefits?

Answer: The $153.10 is the minimum that can be paid to you, even if your earnings were very, very slight.

Question: How do I apply for disability benefits?

Answer: Apply at your Social Security office as soon as possible after the disability. If you can't leave home, make your

Beneficiary	Size of monthly benefit if your answer to Step 3 was:										
	$923 or less	$3,000	$5,000	$7,000	$8,000	$9,000	$10,000	$12,000	$13,000
Disabled worker	153.10	316.40	431.60	546.50	606.30	640.80	671.80	731.50	759.10
Disabled worker & spouse at 62	153.30	435.10	593.50	751.50	833.70	881.10	923.80	1005.90	1043.80
Disabled widow or widower at 50	76.60	158.30	215.90	273.40	303.30	320.50	336.00	365.90	379.60
Disabled worker, wife under 65 & 1 child (fam. max)	153.30	474.50	647.30	820.20	909.30	962.20	1007.80	1097.00	1129.90

The maximum family benefit for a young disabled worker and his or her family in 1981 is $970.50 per month.

application by telephone. If you are hospitalized or are unable to leave home because of the disability, your Social Security office can send a representative to visit you.

Question: Do I have to bring any papers or documents with me when I apply?

Answer: To support your application, you must provide medical evidence—usually a medical report from your physician, or from the hospital, clinic or other health facility where you have been treated. Your Social Security office will help you obtain these reports. Your physician or hospital or other facility will be asked to explain what your disability is, how severe it is, what medical tests have disclosed and what treatment you have received. They will not, however, be asked to decide if you meet the Social Security definition of "disabled." Your Social Security office will send the report to an agency in your state, usually associated with the Vocational Rehabilitation Agency, where it will be reviewed to see if you can be considered disabled. If more information is needed, the agency may ask you to supply it or submit to a medical examination at government expense.

Question: Who pays for the initial report I have to provide?

Answer: Effective December, 1980, the Social Security Administration will pay a reasonable charge for medical reports it needs and requests.

Question: What kind of people are going to be deciding whether I can be considered disabled?

Answer: The review agency is made up of specially trained people, including a physician and a disability-evaluation specialist.

Question: How soon after I apply will the benefits begin?

Answer: Benefits begin after a waiting period of five full calendar months. However, if you are disabled for more than six full months before you apply, back payments may be available, but not before the sixth full month of disability. And back payments are limited to the 12 months preceding the month in which you apply. So it's important to apply as soon as you become disabled.

Question: My disability lasted for a year and a half, but I've never gotten around to applying for benefits. Can I still get them?

Answer: Yes. You can apply at any time. However, if you have recovered from a disability that lasted at least 12 months and you want to collect back payments, you will not be eligible for them if you wait longer than 14 months after you recover before you apply.

Question: I was disabled when I was in junior high school. My father will start getting retirement benefits shortly. Will I have to wait five months before I can collect my benefits as a disabled dependent?

Answer: No. If you are disabled before age 22 you can get benefits beginning with the month your parent starts collecting retirement or disability benefits or dies.

Question: I submitted my application for disability benefits yesterday. How do I find out if my application has been approved?

Answer: The Social Security Administration will send you a notice as soon as a decision has been reached.

Question: What happens if my application is denied?

Answer: The notice you get from the Social Security Administration will give you the reason. Perhaps the review agency decided that your condition is not serious enough, or is not likely to last for 12 months or more. Perhaps you have not worked long enough or recently enough.

Question: My application was denied, but I don't agree with the decision. What should I do?

Answer: If you can present new evidence about your disability—or even if you have no new evidence—your Social Security office will see that your case is reconsidered. If your application is again rejected, you can request a hearing before a hearing examiner of the Social Security Administration. You will not have to pay for the hearing or for having your case reconsidered. If the hearing examiner decides against you, you can take the case to the appeals council of the Social Security Administration in Washington, D.C. If the appeals council rules against you, you can take your case to Federal court.

Question: My application for disability benefits was denied, and I'm not planning to appeal. But does the fact that my claim was denied mean that I can't get other Social Security benefits?

Answer: No.

Question: Is it true that I can get rehabilitation and job assistance if I'm disabled?

Answer: Yes. When you apply for Social Security disability benefits, you will also be considered for vocational rehabilitation by your state's vocational-rehabilitation agency, regardless of whether your application for benefits is ultimately approved or rejected. You can also get job counseling and special job-placement services from your state's employment service.

Question: Will I have to pay for the rehabilitation services?

Answer: No. These services generally are paid with Federal and state funds or, in some cases, with funds from the Social Security Administration.

Question: Why would the Social Security Administration want to pay for rehabilitation services when it must also pay disability benefits?

Answer: The administration expects to save money by rehabilitating beneficiaries because it anticipates that the cost of rehabilitation in the long run will be less than the cost of paying benefits.

Question: I applied for disability benefits and was found eligible, but really don't want to undergo any rehabilitation right now. Can I refuse?

Answer: Yes, but you will not receive any benefits if you have no good cause for refusing the rehabilitation services.

Question: How long will my disability benefits be paid?

Answer: As a disabled worker, you can continue to collect as long as you are unable to work.

Question: I'm drawing disability benefits but am also managing to do some work. Will this affect my benefits?

Answer: If you are receiving benefits as a disabled worker, as an adult disabled from childhood, or as a disabled widow or widower, in most cases you are exempt from the general rule under which some benefits are withheld if you have substantial earnings, but you are exempt only as long as you remain disabled. In other words your annual earnings while you are receiving benefits are not considered in determining the amount of your benefit.

Question: Will the benefits my dependents collect because of my disability be affected by their earnings?

Answer: Some of your dependents' benefits may be withheld if they are not disabled and earn more than $4,080 in a year. In general $1 in benefits will be withheld for each $2 a dependent earns over $4,080. For the first year in which a dependent receives benefits, he or she will receive a full benefit for any month in which no more than $340 is earned or not substantial services are performed in self-employment. After the first year, benefits are withheld if more than $4,080 is earned even if he or she did not earn wages or perform substantial services every month. ("Substantial" is interpreted as 45 hours of work or more in a month or, in some cases, as little as 15 hours. Consult your Social Security office to see what applies in your case.)

Question: I've been collecting disability benefits for about a year, but am recovering fast now and hope to return to work. Do I have to keep the Social Security Administration posted?

Answer: Yes. If your condition improves or if you return to work, no matter how little you earn, the law requires you to tell your Social Security office. Whenever medical evidence indicates that you are no longer disabled, your payments will continue for a three-month period of adjustment, then will stop. The three-month period begins with the month in which you ceased to be disabled.

Question: I'm not completely recovered yet, but want to go back to work anyway, even though I'm not sure I'm up to it. I figure I'll never know until I try. But will I risk losing my disability benefits?

Answer: No. If you are a disabled worker, or a person disabled in childhood, and you go back to work despite your disability, you will get a nine-month trial work period during which you will continue to collect your benefits (the nine months don't have to be consecutive). If after nine months you appear able to do substantial gainful work, you will continue to collect benefits for a three-month adjustment period, after which the payments will stop. If it is decided, after nine months, that you cannot do substantial gainful work, you will continue to collect benefits as before. And if at any time during the nine months you recover so markedly that you cease to be disabled, your benefits will stop after a three-month adjustment period, even though your trial work period isn't over yet. As of December, 1980, an extended period of eligibility is provided for persons who have completed nine months of trial work and still continue to have a disabling condition. This period can continue for an additional 15 months.

Question: I'm a disabled widow, not a disabled worker, but I too would like to try to work. Am I eligible for a trial work period?

Answer: Yes. As of December 1980 a change in the law now allows disabled widows and widowers to have a trial work period.

Question: I was disabled for three years but finally was able to go back to work. It went pretty well for a while, but now I've become disabled again. Can I get my disability benefits again?

Answer: Yes. If you become disabled a second time within five years after your benefits as a disabled worker were stopped because you went back to work or ceased being disabled, your benefits can resume with the first full month in which you are again disabled. If you are a disabled widow, a disabled widower, a disabled surviving divorced wife or a person disabled before age 22, you can collect your benefits again if the new disability occurs within seven years after your first payments stopped. However, there is a five-month waiting period for disabled surviving divorced wives and people disabled before age 22. And no one who becomes disabled again can get a trial work period.

Question: Can I collect disability benefits and regular Social Security benefits at the same time?

Answer: No. If you qualify for both, you'll generally receive the payment that is larger.

Question: My husband had been disabled for about seven months when he died. For some reason, we'd never gotten around to applying for disability benefits. Can I apply for back payment benefits now, even though my husband is dead?

Answer: Yes, but you must do so within three months after his death.

Question: My son was born disabled. What disability rules apply to him?

Answer: If he has worked at least 6 quarters before age 24, he is eligible for benefits on his own work record. If he has no work record, benefits are payable to him as early as 18 years of age when a parent (or a grandparent under special circumstances) receives Social Security retirement or disability benefits or when an insured parent dies. In addition, disabled children may be eligible for Supplemental Security Income benefits at any age if they meet certain income and resource requirements—even if their parents are working. If you think your child may qualify, contact your Social Security office.

Question: My daughter is disabled (she wasn't born that way; she was maimed in an accident). When can she start getting benefits?

Answer: If your daughter (or son) is unmarried, is 18 years old or older and became disabled before age 18 and is still disabled, she (or he) can start collecting childhood-disability benefits when you start collecting Social Security retirement or disability benefits, or when you die, provided you have enough work credit under Social Security to cover payments to survivors. Your daughter will not need any Social Security work credit of her own to collect, and her benefits will continue for as long as she is disabled.

Question: Who decides if my children are disabled according to the Social Security definition?

Answer: The procedure is the same as for a worker. A medical report must be submitted and a special state agency reviews the application, then makes the decision.

Question: I had to stop work because of blindness. Will I get disability benefits for this?

Answer: Yes, but the rules vary, depending on your age. If you are 55 to 65 years old and have worked long enough under Social Security to be fully insured, you can collect disability benefits if you are unable to do work requiring abilities or skills comparable to those required by the work you did before you reached 55 or became blind, whichever is later. But you will not receive benefits for any month in which you do manage some substantial gainful work. If you are less than 55 years old, you can collect only if you are unable to do ANY substantial gainful work.

Question: Do I have to be totally, absolutely blind to qualify for these benefits?

Answer: No. The Social Security Administration considers you blind if your vision is not better than 20/200, even with glasses, or if you have a limited visual field of 20 degrees or less.

DISABILITY BENEFITS

Question: I became blind when I was 58. Now that I'm 63 and nearing retirement, it has occurred to me that my retirement benefits will probably be reduced because my earnings have been so low all these years I've been blind. Is that true—are my benefits going to be reduced because of my blindness?

Answer: No. If you have enough work credit under Social Security, and even if you keep working despite your disability, you are eligible for what the Social Security Administration calls a "disability freeze." This means that your future benefits will not be reduced because you have little or no earnings during the years you are disabled.

Question: I thought there was some rule that said blind people had to have a substantial amount of recent work if they wanted to collect benefits. Has this rule been changed?

Answer: Yes. Now blind people need only be fully insured. If you are blind and were refused benefits under the old rule, contact your Social Security office to see if you are now eligible.

Question: I am entitled to workmen's compensation as well as Social Security. How does that affect my benefits?

Answer: If you are a disabled worker under age 62, the total monthly payments to you and your family may not exceed 80% of your average monthly earnings before you became disabled. Your _full_ earnings, including any amounts above the maximum creditable for Social Security, may be considered when your average earnings are figured for this purpose. Social Security benefits are reduced if the combined benefits would be over this limit.

Question: I am a disabled divorcee. My ex-husband passed away recently. Am I eligible for survivor's benefits based on my ex-husband's earnings?

Answer: Yes, if you were married to your former husband for at least 10 years.

Question: I know that in most households it's the man who does the work. But our case was different because I became disabled. We needed income, so my wife went to work, and she was still working when she died. Can I as a disabled widower get benefits based on my wife's earnings?

Answer: Yes.

Question: How early can a disabled person whose spouse has died start to get disability payments?

Answer: As early as age 50 if you are disabled and are the widow, widower or, under certain conditions, the surviving divorced wife of a wage earner with sufficient work credit under Social Security. But your benefits will be permanently reduced if you decide to collect early, with the size of the reduction depending on the age at which you begin collecting.

Question: My spouse, who really enjoyed being the "breadwinner" in the family, died not long after I became disabled. Can I collect benefits based on my spouse's earnings even though I have no work credit of my own?

Answer: Yes.

Question: My husband has been dead for about 10 years. I became disabled in the spring of this year. Can I get disability benefits on my husband's work record even though so much time has passed since his death?

Answer: Probably not. In most cases, you cannot collect unless you become disabled before your spouse died or within seven years after the death. But if you are receiving benefits as a widow with children, you will be eligible if you become disabled before those benefits end or within seven years after they end. The seven-year period is intended to give you a chance to earn enough Social Security work credits to qualify for your own disability benefits.

Question: Two of my children are disabled and have been receiving their child's benefits. But my boy will be 18 next year and his payments are scheduled to stop—or can he keep collecting them?

Answer: He may be able to get benefits past the age of 18

on the basis of his disability. Contact your Social Security office a few months before your son's 18th birthday.

Question: I'm the perennial pessimist. I have this terrible fear that I'll probably become disabled before I reach retirement age and before I've had a chance to get in enough work to be fully insured. Or will different rules apply if this happens to me?

Answer: If you become disabled before you reach retirement age, you will be considered fully insured if you have credit for one-quarter year of work for each year after 1950 up to the year you became disabled. (Do not count the years before you were age 22.) However, you must have credit for at least one and a half years of work.

Question: My life has had its ups and downs. I was disabled as a child, but recovered, only to become disabled again last fall. Can my benefits be restarted?

Answer: Yes, if your second disability occurred within seven years after your first one ended.

Question: I was among the P.O.W.'s released from Vietnam. I could tell you a whole story about that, but for now my problem is this—I was gravely wounded when my plane was shot down and I was taken into captivity, and I've been disabled ever since. Can I get disability benefits for my ordeal?

Answer: Yes. You, or any Vietnam veteran, will be considered for the benefits if your condition prevents you from doing any substantial gainful work and has lasted (or is expected to last) for at least 12 months, or is expected to result in death. (These are the rules that apply to all disabled workers.) Even if you were disabled very early in the war, you may be eligible for up to a year's back payments.

Question: When my child, who is disabled, gets married, will the benefits my child gets be cut off?

Answer: Yes, unless your child marries a person receiving Social Security benefits.

Question: If my spouse gets disabled, can I collect benefits even if we just got married?

Answer: Generally, the wife or dependent husband of a person entitled to disability (or retirement) benefits cannot collect until the marriage has lasted at least one year, unless the couple have a child.

Question: How long must I be disabled before I can obtain Medicare coverage?

Answer: You must be receiving disability benefits for 24 months to qualify for Medicare. These months do not have to be consecutive.

Question: If my benefits cease because I return to work, what happens to my Medicare coverage?

Answer: Medicare coverage, as of December 1980, can continue for three years after benefits stop because of a return to substantial gainful activity.

Question: I was entitled to Medicare when I was receiving disability benefits last year. I am now working and not receiving benefits. How do I qualify for Medicare again if I have to stop work because my disability gets worse?

Answer: As of December 1980, Medicare protection resumes immediately if you start receiving disability benefits again within five years after they ended.

SURVIVORS' BENEFITS

It is an often repeated and well-known statistic that nine out of ten workers who retire are covered to some extent by Social Security. But there is another statistic, equally imposing, that fewer people know about: 95 out of 100 young children and their mothers have extremely valuable life insurance protection under Social Security.

More than 3 million children who have lost a parent and about three quarters of a million widows and widowers are collecting monthly Social Security benefits for survivors. It is not unusual for Social Security survivor's insurance to be the most valuable "asset" a young family has.

The amount of protection depends on the number and age of the children and the earnings of their parents. The earnings of the worker determine the benefit rate. Each child and the widow or widower are entitled to a benefit equal to three-fourths of a retired worker's benefit up to the maximum payable for a family. Benefits are payable to children during the time that they will be least able to support themselves and to a parent who chooses to stay home and care for a child under 18.

THE $100,000 INSURANCE POLICY

A worker who earned the male median amount and died in 1977 at age 35 with a wife 32 years old and two children, three and five, would have left his family the Social Security equivalent of an estate worth $129,265! If he had been earning the maximum, the equivalent would be an estate or insurance of $158,431. Even a comparable worker earning only the Federal minimum wage would have an estate of $79,163.

And the amount of this protection increases automatically as wages and prices go up. In January 1982, the value of the protection for families of the same age composition as given in the previous examples would be $142,163 for the worker earning the median wage for male workers, $196,791 for the worker earning the maximum, and $87,950 for the worker earning the Federal minimum wage.

Under Social Security, the protection provided is not a fixed-dollar life insurance policy. Benefit protection for the contributor increases as the individual's earnings go up, and in addition the benefits being paid are automatically increased as prices rise.

WHO GETS THE BENEFITS?

Children benefit primarily on the death of a parent. Widowed mothers and fathers who are taking care of young children of the deceased wage earners also benefit. A monthly payment is made to a child on the death of either parent, if that parent is fully or currently insured. Therefore, if a man and a wife have each worked enough to meet the insured status requirements, a benefit to the child is paid if either one dies.

Payments are made until age 18 and are continued to age 22 for full-time students. Payments are continued in adulthood for children who were totally disabled before age 22. These payments continue for a lifetime unless at some point the beneficiary recovers enough to be able to work.

Payments to widows and widowers before age 60 are made only if they have in their care a child of the deceased wage earner who is entitled to benefits. Their own benefits, but not the child's, are reduced if they work and earn amounts that exceed the exemption in the "retirement" or "earnings" test for those below 65. This test applies to each person receiving a survivor's benefit in the same way as to a retired worker.

The surviving child is considered to have suffered a loss of income if either working parent dies—a loss that is not made up for by the continuing work of the other parent. Also, if the surviving widow remarries before age 60, her benefit stops, but the child's does not.

DEFERRED LIFE INSURANCE BENEFITS

Elderly widows, widowers, and dependent parents also receive benefits as a result of the death of a wage earner. The widow or widower not only has a right to benefits as long as there are young children, but also a right to a deferred benefit payable at age 60 or later—a right which is part of the life insurance protection, or survivor's benefits of Social Security.

Part of the value of Social Security survivor benefits for young families is the deferred annuity payable to the widow in old age. There is protection for the widow or widower up until the time the youngest child reaches age 18 (only the child collects benefits if he stays in school until age 22), then benefits can begin again when the widow or widower reaches age 60.

Certain benefits for disabled people—disabled widows and widowers as well as, in some cases, disabled children over 18— are also payable because of the death of a wage earner and are therefore survivor's benefits. They are paid for out of the old-age and survivor's insurance trust fund, not the disability insurance trust fund.

LUMP SUM PAYMENT AT DEATH OF WORKER

A lump sum is paid to help survivors meet the special expenses connected with the last illness and death of the worker. The continuing monthly benefit is designed to make up in part for the loss of the earnings of the wage earner, but the lump sum is meant to help meet the immediate expenses connected with death. The amount is low—$255. Specifically, the law provides for a payment of three times the primary insurance amount, but with a maximum of $255. This provision has not been updated for a long time, and since benefit rates have been substantially increased, the $255 ceiling is now less than three times the primary insurance amount in all cases.

This benefit is payable on the death of any insured wage earner whether or not he is survived by a person eligible for monthly benefits. If the wage earner is survived by a widow or widower, the payment is generally made to that individual. If not, the payment may be made directly to a funeral director or divided among those who have taken responsibility for providing for the burial of the deceased.

WIDOW'S BENEFITS

Even if there are no dependent children when a husband dies, the widow can collect benefits when she reaches age 60.

The amount of monthly payment will depend on your age when you start getting benefits and the amount your deceased husband would have been entitled to or was receiving when he died.

Widow's benefits range from 71½ per cent of the deceased husband's benefit amount at age 60 to 100 per cent at 65. If you start receiving benefits at age 65, you will get 100 per cent of the amount your husband would be receiving if he were still alive.

If you're disabled, you can get widow's benefits as early as age 50, but the payment will be reduced.

If you are entitled to retirement benefits on your own work record and you receive reduced widow's benefits between age 50 and 62, your own retirement benefit at 65 also would be reduced.

IF YOU REMARRY

Ordinarily, a widow loses her Social Security rights when she remarries. But, benefits to a widow or widower who remarries at 60 or older can continue without any reduction in the amount.

If your spouse gets Social Security checks, however, you can take a wife's (or husband's) benefit on his (or her) record if it would be larger than your widow's (or widower's) payment.

IF YOU DIVORCE

You may also get payments if your ex-husband dies, provided you are 60 or older (50, if you're disabled) and you were married ten years or more or you have young children entitled to benefits on his record.

MEDICARE FOR WIDOWS

If you are 50 or older, and you become disabled while getting checks because you have young children in your care, contact Social Security about eligibility for Medicare. Even though you haven't filed a claim for payments based on the disability (since you are already getting payments as a mother), you could be eligible for Medicare protection if you have been disabled for two years or longer.

BENEFITS AND PUBLIC PENSIONS

Social Security benefits payable to spouses, widows and widowers may be reduced by the amount of any pension or annuity he or she receives based on work in non-covered public employment.

However, the offset does not apply if the spouse, widow or widower would be eligible for public pension before December 1982, as long as he or she also qualifies for Social Security dependent's benefits under the law in effect on January 1, 1977.

FULL LIFE INSURANCE

Any worker who has contributed long enough to be either fully insured or currently insured has life insurance protection under Social Security. Fully insured is the same for life insurance protection as for retirement benefits.

So, to be fully insured at the time of death, a wage earner needs to have had one quarter of coverage for each year elapsing after 1950, or age 21 if later, up to the year in which he dies, becomes totally disabled, or becomes 62, with a minimum of six quarters of coverage and a maximum of 40. But, additionally, a worker who is not fully insured may be protected for life insurance payable to the children and their mother, with six quarters of coverage during the 13-quarter period ending with the quarter of death.

QUESTIONS AND ANSWERS

Question: As a widow, I'm told that the amount of benefits I can collect on the basis of my late husband's earnings will depend on how soon I begin collecting and on how soon my husband began collecting before he died. Could you give me a breakdown of these figures?

Answer: Yes. If your husband did not begin collecting his benefits until he was 65 years old, or if he died before he was 65, and you wait until you are 65 years old, you will receive 100 per cent of what you husband was entitled to get at age 65. If you begin collecting before you are age 65, but you husband did not, you will get your husband's age-65 benefits, minus 5.7 percentage points for each year under 65, down to a minimum of 71.5 per cent of your husband's age-65 benefits if you start collecting at age 60.

If you wait until you are age 65, but your husband had been getting reduced benefits because he did not wait, you will get 100 per cent of the reduced benefits your husband had been getting. And if you begin collecting before age 65 and your husband did the same, you will get either your husband's reduced amount or his age-65 amount, minus the necessary reductions because of your earlier age, whichever is lower.

Question: What's the earliest age at which I can start collecting my late husband's benefits?

Answer: If you have no children, the earliest age is 60, unless you are disabled, in which case the minimum age is 50. If you are caring for unmarried children under age 18, or for a disabled child age 18 or older who become disabled before age 22, you can collect even if you are less than 60 years old.

Question: I'm younger than 60 and have been receiving

benefits from my late husband's earnings because my two girls are under 18. What happens when they turn 18?

Answer: Your payments stop when your youngest daughter becomes 18 years old, unless one of your children is disabled or becomes disabled before age 22.

Question: I'm a 48-year-old widow. I was able to start collecting benefits right away when my husband died because I had our young children in my care. But when our children reached 18 (the youngest one turned 18 last winter), the benefits stopped. But I'm still a widow nonetheless. When will I be able to start getting survivor's benefits of my own?

Answer: You can resume collecting benefits when you reach age 60, if you have not remarried, or when you reach age 50 if you are disabled.

Question: Could you give me a rundown of all the people who might be eligible for survivor's benefits when a person dies?

Answer: Briefly, survivor's benefits can be paid to a widow or widower age 60 or older; to a disabled widow as early as age 50; to a widow or widower at any age who is caring for unmarried children under age 18 or for disabled children; unmarried dependent children under age 18; unmarried dependent full-time students under age 22; to dependent parents if they are age 62 or older, and, under certain conditions, to a surviving divorced wife.

Question: If someone in our family who has worked under Social Security dies how should we arrange to get the benefits?

Answer: A member of the family should go to your Social Security office. If you are hospitalized or unable to leave the house, you should write or telephone the office. The staff there can arrange to have a representative visit you.

Question: How soon after the death should we apply for benefits?

Answer: As soon as possible. In some cases there are no

SURVIVORS' BENEFITS

back benefits payable and when there are, back payments can be made for no more than 12 months. Therefore, if you wait longer than that, you may lose some benefits.

Question: When I apply for survivor's benefits, will I need to bring any papers with me?

Answer: Your Social Security office can tell you what documents you need.

Question: I've heard you can get a lump-sum payment when a worker dies. How does this work?

Answer: The insured worker's widow or widower, at any age, can collect a lump-sum death benefit if the spouse's death certificate is presented and if the application is filed within two years after the worker's death.

Question: What if the worker dies but leaves no spouse? Who gets the death benefits then?

Answer: The person who pays the dead worker's burial expenses can collect the lump-sum death payment, but he must present a receipted funeral bill and the death certificate.

Question: My husband and I had a lot of difficulties and so we were divorced. He passed away recently. Am I eligible for benefits based on his earnings, even though we weren't married at the time he died?

Answer: Yes, if you are at least 60 years old (at least 50 if you are disabled) and were married for at least 10 years before you were divorced. If you are caring for children from your previous marriage who are under 18 or who became disabled before age 22, you can collect before you are 60 years old.

Question: My husband was killed in Vietnam six months after we were married. Can I collect benefits even though we were married for such a short time?

Answer: Yes. Usually you have to be married at least nine months to be eligible for widow's or widower's benefits. However, that time requirement is waived if the insured person's death was accidental or if it occurred in the line of duty while he or she was on active duty as a member of the Armed Forces.

Question: A friend of mine, married just four months, was able to collect benefits because her husband died in action in the Korean War. But my husband is no longer in the Armed Forces. How long will our marriage have to last if I am to collect benefits when he dies?

Answer: Generally, a widow, a dependent widower or a step-child of a worker cannot collect survivor's benefits unless the marriage has lasted at least nine months.

Question: If I should die, could my parents collect survivor's benefits?

Answer: Yes, if they are at least 62 years old and were getting at least half of their support from you, and if you were fully insured. Confusion about what constitutes parents' support has snarled many applications. Your Social Security office can advise you.

Question: How much could my parents collect in the event I die?

Answer: If only one of your parents is eligible, that parent could get 82.5 per cent of what your retirement benefit would have been. If both of your parents are eligible, each would get 75 per cent.

Question: Let's say I die tomorrow and am not yet 65 years old. How much credit will I have to have to be fully insured? I ask because I understand that the kinds of benefits my survivors will be eligible for will depend on whether I'm fully or currently insured.

Answer: If you die (or become disabled) before reaching age 65, you will be fully insured if you have one-quarter year of work credit for each year between 1950 and the year you die (or become disabled). Do not count the year before you were age 22. You will need a minimum of one and a half years of work credit.

SURVIVORS' BENEFITS

Question: I've always valued my freedom, and so I never got married. What if I die the day before my Social Security payments are scheduled to start? Since I have no dependents, will I have lost everything?

Answer: Yes.

Question: How much will my children get if I die?

Answer: Regardless of whether you were fully insured or currently insured, and regardless of whether you are their father or their working mother, each child can collect 75 per cent of the retirement benefit you would have been entitled to up to the family maximum payable.

Question: My wife and I both work. If both of us should die, would our children collect from both of our work records, or what?

Answer: Your children would collect on the basis of whoever earned more, you or your wife. However, if you have so many children that the family maximum on either record was reached before full benefits were payable to all of them, the records could be combined to provide additional benefits.

Question: My dad always said his dream was for me to go to college, and that's what I did. He died recently (I'm sorry he'll miss my graduation) and I've been getting my survivor's benefits. The checks are supposed to stop when I reach 22, but my 22nd birthday is going to fall right in the middle of the semester. Can I get them extended to the end of the semester?

Answer: If you are a full-time student, and have not filled your undergraduate degree requirements, your payments will not stop the day you reach 22, but will continue to the end of the semester or quarter in which your birthday occurs. If your school is not on the semester or quarter system, your payments will continue until you finish the course or until two months after the month you reach age 22, whichever comes first.

Question: In our home the roles were somewhat switched, with my wife doing most of the working, particularly as we got older. Now that she has passed on, I'd like to know what I must do to qualify for survivor's benefits.

Answer: You must be at least 60 years old. And your wife must have been fully insured. The amount you will receive will depend on how many years under age 65 you are when you begin collecting.

Question: When my wife died I was left with two children to raise. But my wife had been a working woman and had credits under Social Security. Can I collect "father's benefits," the same way my wife would have collected "mother's benefits" if I had been the one who died?

Answer: In December 1973, federal court in New Jersey overturned a Social Security rule that would have barred these benefits to men like you whose working wives died and left them with children to care for. The previous rule permitted payments to the children only. Now you as well will be eligible for the same payments your wife would have collected had you died instead—payments based on the earnings record of the dead spouse.

Question: I'm a widow who has finally decided to get married again. Does that mean I'll lose my survivor's benefits?

Answer: Yes, if you are less than 60 years old, although your dependent children, if you have any, can continue to collect even if your new husband supports or adopts them. If you are more than 60 years old and have no children in your care, your widow's benefits will not be reduced or terminated. If your wife's benefits are larger than your widow's benefits, you will receive the greater amount.

SUPPLEMENTAL SECURITY INCOME

There have been in recent years a number of governmental assistance programs designed to help lower-income people meet the expenses of living. Some of these programs are designed for special purposes, such as the Medicaid program which is jointly financed by the Federal government and the state governments who administer the program. The Federal government also pays for housing supplements, subsidized public housing, legal aid, various social services and some public service jobs on a need-basis.

THE AFDC PROGRAM

The Aid to Families with Dependent Children Program (AFDC) is principally for needy mothers with children and is generally what we mean when we refer to "welfare." It is a program administered by the states, the state deciding on the level of assistance paid and the conditions of eligibility in accordance with broad standards established by Federal law. There are some Federal funds available for this program.

FOOD STAMPS, TAX CREDITS, OTHER BENEFITS

The Federally-run Food Stamp Program is another program designed to bolster inadequate family income, as are temporary tax credits for low-income families for children. The Veterans' Administration also provides veterans' pensions for needy, disabled and elderly veterans and the families of deceased veterans. This VA program is completely separate from retirement benefits due career service personnel, and is available to veterans on a need-basis only.

SUPPLEMENTAL SECURITY INCOME

By far the broadest of these Federally assisted programs is the Supplemental Security Income (SSI) Program, run by Social Security, for the aged, blind, and disabled. SSI began operation in January 1974 and together with state supplementation took the place of the Federal-state programs of Old Age Assistance, Aid to the Blind, and Aid to the Permanently and Totally Disabled. State supplementation is required in some cases by Federal law.

THE GOALS OF SSI

SSI is a Federal program that pays monthly checks to people in financial need who are 65 or older and to people in need at any age who are blind or disabled.

The aim of the program is to provide monthly checks when they are needed so that anyone who is 65 or older or blind or disabled can have a basic cash income — $348 a month for one person and $357 for a married couple, effective July 1980.

This doesn't mean that every eligible person gets that much in his or her SSI check every month. Some people get less because they already have other income. Some people get more because they live in a state that adds money to the Federal payment.

In most states, a person who is eligible for SSI is also eligible for Medicaid and social services provided by the state.

WHO IS ELIGIBLE?

People who have little or no regular cash income and do not own much property or things that can be turned into cash, such as stocks, bonds, jewelry, or other valuables, may get SSI.

In addition, eligibility for checks based on blindness or disability depends on the severity of the condition.

To be considered disabled, a person must be unable to perform gainful work because of a physical or mental impairment which has lasted (or is expected to last) for at least 12 months or which can be expected to result in death.

Blindness under the SSI program is defined as central visual acuity of 20/200 or less in the better eye with the use of a corrective lens or visual field restriction of 20 degrees or less.

There is no specific work requirement to receive SSI, and indeed, you can collect even if you have never worked.

PROPERTY REQUIREMENTS

A person who is single (or married but not living with his or her spouse) can have assets worth up to $1,500 and still get checks. The amount for a couple is $2,250. Assets include savings accounts, stocks, bonds, jewelry, and other valuables a person or couple own.

Not everything owned counts as an asset. A home doesn't count. And the Federal government does not ask for liens on the homes of people who get SSI.

Personal effects, household goods, insurance policies, or a car may not count either, depending on their value.

INCOME REQUIREMENTS

People can have some money coming in and still get SSI. The first $20 a month in income generally isn't counted. Income above the first $20 a month (apart from earnings) generally reduces the amount of the SSI check. This includes Social Security checks, veteran's compensation, worker's compensation, pensions, annuities, gifts, and other income.

People who work while they are getting SSI can earn as much as $65 a month without any reduction in their SSI checks. The check is reduced $1 for each $2 in earnings over $65 in a month.

For eligible people who live in someone else's household—a son's or daughter's home, for example—the SSI check may be reduced.

NOT SOCIAL SECURITY

Supplemental Security Income is not the same as Social Security, even though the program is run by the Social Security Administration. The money for SSI comes from general funds of the United States Treasury. Social Security benefits are paid from contributions of wokers, employers, and self-employed people. Social Security funds are not used for SSI checks.

People who get Social Security checks can get SSI checks, too, if they are eligible for both. But, a person does not have to be eligible for Social Security to get SSI.

HOW MUCH IS RECEIVED?

The amount of an SSI check depends on how much income there is, living arrangements, and other circumstances that affect financial needs. In future years, the amount of SSI payment will increase automatically to keep pace with changes in the cost of living. These automatic increases will generally be included in the July check. If the amount of the check will change, recipients will get a notice explaining the change.

RECEIVING CHECKS

SSI payments are made in gold-colored U.S. government checks. A notice of eligibility explains when checks will begin and in what amount.

Checks usually arrive in the mail about the same date at the beginning of each month. If the first of the month is a Saturday,

Sunday, or a legal holiday, checks will be received on the Friday before.

CHECKS NOT DUE

If you receive a check you know is not due you, return it to the U.S. Treasury Department, Division of Disbursement, at the address shown on the envelope in which it was delivered. Include a note telling why you are returning it. Or, take it to any Social Security office. They will return it for you and give you a receipt.

DIRECT DEPOSIT

You may have checks deposited directly in your checking or savings account in a bank, savings bank, savings and loan association or similar institution, or Federal- or state-chartered credit union.

The advantages of direct deposit are:

You don't have to stand in line to cash or deposit your check.

If you're away from home, your money is available in your account instead of sitting in your mailbox.

You don't have any problem cashing your check because it goes directly into your account.

You don't have to worry about losing your check or having it stolen.

To arrange for direct deposit, contact the financial organization you choose and ask for a direct deposit form SF-1199. Completion of the form only authorizes deposits into your account. Only you or those authorized by you may make withdrawals.

RECEIVING SOCIAL SERVICES

People getting Federal SSI checks, or state supplemental checks, are also eligible for social services provided by the state. These services help people meet problems in daily living or special problems related to age or a handicapping condition.

Your Social Security office can tell you about services available in your area and put you in touch with the office that can help you.

REPRESENTATION

You have the right to be represented by an attorney, or another person you choose in any business you have with Social Security. This does not necessarily mean you will need a representative. Most people handle their business themselves with the help of the people in the Social Security office. However, if you wish to be represented, Social Security will be glad to work with your representative just as it would work with you.

There are special regulations concerning who may represent you, what your representative may do, and how much he or she may charge for services.

REMAINING ELIGIBLE FOR SSI

Every SSI case is reviewed once a year to make sure that people getting checks are still eligible and that they are being paid the correct amount. These reviews are required by law. This may be done by a questionnaire, telephone or personal interview at home or in the Social Security office.

Do not wait for Social Security to contact you if there has been a change in your circumstances. Report any change.

If you report all changes promptly, adjustments can be made quickly. Failure to report may result in an overpayment which must be repaid, or you could miss out on extra money if a change in circumstances means a bigger check.

Failure to report a change or false statements are penalized but there will be no penalty if you couldn't help reporting late or if you failed to report but it wasn't your fault.

HOW TO REPORT

Reports can be made by telephone, mail, or in person, whichever is easiest. If reports are made in writing these details should be included:

Name of the claimant.
The Social Security claim number under which payment is made.
Change being reported.
Date it occurred.
Signature and address.
Report forms are available at any Social Security office.

YOU MUST REPORT IF:

1. *You move or change your address*, even if your checks are deposited directly in a bank or other financial institution for you.

2. *There is a change in your household*, and you and your husband or wife separate or, if you are separated now, begin to live together again. Also report if you begin living in someone else's home or move out of someone else's home.

Report if you begin living with others and share in the household expenses. And if there are any changes in the amount you or others contribute to expenses.

Also if there is a change in the number of people who live with you.

3. *You enter or leave an institution* — a residential institution, hospital, skilled nursing facility, nursing home. intermediate care facility, or correctional institution. Your notice should give the name of the institution and the date entered or were released. If unable to report, ask someone in the institution's office to help you.

4. *You plan to leave the United States* for a period of 30 or more consecutive days. Report in advance and give the date you plan to leave and the date of your return.

You are not eligible to receive an SSI check for any full month you are outside the U.S. Once you have been outside the U.S. for 30 or more consecutive days, checks cannot start again until you have been back in the U.S. for at least 30 consecutive days.

5. *You marry or your marriage ends.*

6. *Your income changes.* If you have income other than your SSI checks, promptly report any change in the amount. Your right to SSI checks, or the amount of your checks, may be affected by changes in the amount of other income.

If you are married, you also should report any change in your husband's or wife's income.

If a child under 18 (or student under 12) living with parents is getting SSI checks, any change in the income of a parent must be reported, too.

If you also get Social Security checks, you *do not* have to report when there is a general benefit increase. Any necessary adjustment will be made automatically.

Under SSI, income includes anything you receive. It even includes items you would not have to report for Federal, state, or local income taxes. It includes wages you receive as an employee, whether in cash or otherwise; any net earnings from self-employment in a trade or business; food, shelter, clothing, and funds to help pay for them; VA compensation or VA pension and any other benefits to veterans; railroad retirement and railroad unemployment benefits; annuities, pensions from any government or private source, worker's compensation, unemployment insurance benefits, black lung benefits, and Social Security benefits.

It also includes prizes, settlements, and awards, including court-ordered awards; proceeds of life insurance policies; gifts and contributions in cash or otherwise; support and alimony payments; inheritances in cash or property; rents and interest; and strike pay and other benefits from unions.

7. *There is a change in your resources.* For example, if you (or your spouse) buy or become the owner of any additional real estate, buy or become the owner of a car or other additional personal property, sell any real estate, sell a car or other personal property. You must also report if you or your spouse adds to your savings account or invests money in some other manner.

8. *You are blind or disabled and there is a change in your condition.* Payments will stop if your disability ends or your sight is restored, but even if your condition improves to the extent you are no longer considered disabled or blind, payments will be made for a temporary adjustment period. Report immediately if you are blind and working and your working expenses change.

9. *You are a student under 22* and you start or stop attending school regularly.

10. *A drug addict or alcoholic stops treatment.* Whoever is responsible for handling SSI checks for a recipient who has been

medically determined a drug addict or alcoholic must report promptly if the recipient stops undergoing treatment. Drug addicts and alcoholics can get SSI checks only as long as they continue with required treatment.

11. *A recipient can't manage his affairs.* Sometimes a person getting SSI checks loses the mental or physical ability to manage the money. When this happens, the person who takes care of the recipient must report. Arrangements will be made to issue checks to a relative or other person who can act for the recipient. This person is called a "representative payee."

12. *A recipient dies or any other person in the household dies.*

RIGHT TO QUESTION DECISIONS MADE ON SSI CLAIMS

When Social Security makes a decision about your eligibility for SSI checks, that SSI checks will stop, or that the amount you get will be changed, a written notice is sent. If you don't agree with the decision, you have a right to appeal. There are four steps you can take. The steps generally must be taken in order.

1. *Reconsideration.* First, you may ask Social Security to reconsider your case. There are several kinds of reconsiderations you can request. The people at any Social Security office will help you apply for any of them, though you may have a representative or lawyer apply.

2. *Hearing.* If you disagree with the results of the reconsideration, you may then ask for a hearing before an official of the Office of Hearings and Appeals.

3. *Appeals Council review.* If you disagree with the hearing decision, you may ask for a review of this decision by the Appeals Council.

4. *Federal court action.* If you disagree with the decision of the Appeals Council (or if the Appeals Council declined to review your case), you may then bring a civil action in a Federal court.

Reconsideration

A reconsideration is ordinarily the first step to appeal a decision of Social Security. In any reconsideration, a complete review of your case will be made by someone in the Social Security office who did not take part in the decision being appealed.

To request a reconsideration, you must ask for it within *60 days* from the date you receive the notice of the decision on your case. Phone, write, or visit any Social Security office. The people there will help you with the reconsideration request, which must be in writing.

If Social Security decided your SSI checks would be reduced or stopped, you have a right to have the payments continued unchanged or re-started while your case is being reconsidered. But then you must apply for reconsideration within *10 days*, rather than *60 days*, of the date you received notice.

If checks continue during reconsideration and it is later decided the original decision was correct, you may have to pay back money you were not entitled to.

There are three ways of presenting a case for reconsideration. You can choose the first or second way if you recently applied for SSI and Social Security decided you were either not eligible at all or that the amount of your SSI check is less than you thought it would be.

You can choose any of the three methods if you have been getting SSI checks and the decision is that you are no longer eligible to receive any payments or that the amount should be reduced.

If the dispute involves a medical issue, the reconsideration is handled by the State Disability Determination Services and only a *case review* is available.

If Social Security decided you were no longer disabled enough to receive SSI payments, your first appeal would be a *hearing*.

1. *Case Review*. Under this method, the evidence in your file is given an independent review by someone in the Social Security office who did not take part in the decision you are appealing. While you won't be present during the review, you do have a right to first look at the evidence already in your file. If you wish to see your medical records, however, you must first designate a representative. In some cases, you can get copies of your medical records. And you can add any written or oral evidence you feel would help your case.

2. *Informal Conference*. In addition to your rights under case

review, you also may personally present your reasons for disagreeing with Social Security's decision to the person who will make the reconsideration decision on your case. If you have a representative, he or she may attend the conference. You may bring witnesses to testify for you.

3. *Formal conference.* You have the same rights as under case review and informal conference. In addition, you may ask that Social Security subpoena unwilling witnesses to appear for cross-examination and to bring with them any evidence about your case. A formal conference is available only if you have been getting SSI checks.

A reconsideration decision usually will be made within 15 days after you make a request unless a medical question is involved. If you disagree with the reconsideration decision, you may request a hearing.

Hearing

The person who presides at the hearing is an administrative law judge of the Office of Hearings and Appeals of the Social Security Administration. The presiding judge had no part in the original decision or the reconsideration of your case.

To request a hearing, call, write, or come into the Social Security office within 60 days from the date you receive the notice about the reconsideration. The people at the Social Security office will help you complete the forms for requesting a hearing.

A hearing is usually held in the city where the Social Security office that handles your case is located. You or your representative may attend the hearing, if you wish, and present your case in person. At the hearing, the presiding official will state what issues must be decided. He or she may also ask you (and any witnesses you present) questions about your case. You or your representative may question the witnesses, present new evidence, and examine the evidence that the presiding official will use to make a decision.

If you don't want to attend the hearing, you don't have to. The presiding official will base the decision on all the evidence submitted in your case, plus any additional evidence or statements you submit. After the hearing, a copy of the decision will be sent to you. If you disagree with the decision, you may request a review by the Appeals Council.

Review by the Appeals Council

The Appeals Council is part of the Office of Hearings and Appeals.

A request for an Appeals Council review must be filed within the time limit mentioned in the notice of the hearing decision.

Whether your request for a review of the presiding official's decision will be granted is up to the Appeals Council. If the Appeals Council decides to review your case, you have a right to request an appearance to present oral arguments before the Appeals Council. When the Appeals Council decides your case, a copy of the decision is sent to you. If you disagree with the decision or if the Appeals Council declines to review your case, you may bring a suit in a Federal district court.

QUESTIONS AND ANSWERS

Question: What's this I hear about a guaranteed income for the old, the blind and the disabled?

Answer: You're thinking about the Federal government's Supplemental Security Income program for the aged, blind, and disabled who have limited income and resources.

Question: How much money will these people be receiving?

Answer: The Federal government provides an amount of $238.00 per month for an individual and $357.00 per month for a couple. These are basic amounts. Added to this are varying amounts provided by the states—each state differs in the amount it provides. If an eligible person or a couple is living in another person's household and receiving support and maintenance from that person, the SSI basic amount is reduced by one-third.

Question: The program sounds great—but why is it being done?

Answer: As the name suggests, the program is intended to provide supplemental security money, when it is needed, so that people who are old or blind or disabled can count on a basic cash income.

Question: It sounds even better. But someone's going to have to pay for this. Who?

Answer: The money is taken from general funds of the United States Treasury—from personal income taxes, corporation taxes and other taxes. The Social Security Administration operates the program, but Social Security funds are not used to make the payments.

Question: You said this program was for poor people. How poor do you have to be?

Answer: In general, you must have little or no regular cash income and very little property or other items that can be turned into cash—items such as stocks, bonds or jewelry. Specifically, a single person (or a married person not living with the spouse) can have assets—possessions—worth up to $1,500. The figure for a married couple is $2,250. But not all possessions count as assets. A house, if used as a primary residence, personal effects and household goods, for example, generally don't count. Nor will the government put liens on the houses of those receiving supplemental-security payments. Insurance policies or an automobile may or may not affect eligibility. It depends on their value.

Question: How much income can I have and still qualify for Supplemental Security payments?

Answer: The first $20 per month in income from all sources—Social Security checks, veteran's compensation, pensions, workmen's compensation, gifts, annuities, wages and self-employment earnings, and so on—generally won't affect your payment. Any such income above the $20 generally will reduce it. If you work, your payment won't be affected by your first $65 a month of earned income. Half of what you earn above $65 ($85 if there is no unearned income as well) counts against your payment.

Question: What other conditions affect my eligibility?

Answer: You must be a citizen or an alien lawfully admitted for permanent residency and you must live in one of the 50 states or the District of Columbia.

Question: What kind of disability would make me eligible?

Answer: The Supplemental Security Income definition of disability and blindness generally match Social Security's disability definitions. You are considered disabled if a physical or mental impairment prevents a person from doing any substantial gainful work and is expected to last or has lasted for at least 12 months or is expected to result in death.

Question: I have a 10-year-old child who is disabled. Can I get any benefits for him even though I am not receiving any benefits myself?

Answer: Yes. A child under 18 years of age is considered disabled if he has an impairment that is expected to last at least 12 months and is comparable in severity to one that would prevent an adult from working. However, a parent's income and resources can affect a child's eligibility. You would have to check with your local Social Security office.

Question: Do I need any quarters of coverage to qualify?

Answer: The SSI program is based upon need and does not require any work credits for eligibility.

Question: I think I qualify! How do I apply?

Answer: Go to your Social Security office to file for the benefits.

Question: Can I collect Social Security benefits as well as Supplemental Security Income payments?

Answer: Yes, if you are eligible for both and if the amount of your regular Social Security benefit minus $20 does not exceed the amount you would receive from SSI.

Question: I qualify for the supplemental security payments, but I'm living with my daughter now and hope to stay for as long as she'll have me. Will this affect my payments?

Answer: They may be reduced.

MEDICARE

For people over 65 years of age the advent of Medicare has meant a new freedom from some of the worst fears of old age. We no longer need to fear the illness that could in one sweep wipe out the savings and security of a lifetime.

Today, the advances of modern medicine—replacement arteries, heart valves, limbs and joints—are available to the stricken elderly without the worry of prohibitive cost. Medical treatment that was only for the very rich a few short years ago is today available nationwide.

NOT A PANACEA

But as important as Medicare benefits are, they do not cover the total cost of medical care. For the average insured person, Medicare covers 40 percent of the medical bills. So there are many gaps that must be filled from savings and income or through such additional medical insurance as Blue Cross and Blue Shield.

WHO RECEIVES MEDICARE?

Nearly everyone who is 65 years of age and over and eligible for Social Security receives Medicare free. Even if you are not insured under Social Security you may still be eligible for Medicare if you pay a monthly premium.

YOU ARE ELIGIBLE FOR MEDICARE IF:

* You are 65 or over, unconditionally (even if you are still working and even if you are not insured under Social Security).
* You are disabled (under age 65) and entitled to Social Security benefits for at least 24 months.
* You or your dependents suffer chronic kidney failure for which you require dialysis or transplant. One condition: you must have been insured by Social Security on your job.

With few exceptions, everyone is eligible for Medicare when they turn 65, even if they don't receive Social Security. (Exceptions: aliens, convicted criminals, and some Federal workers.) Government employees usually are covered by separate Federal health plans.

Most eligible people are also insured by Social Security. These people will get Medicare Part A (hospital insurance) completely free of charge. Medicare Part B (medical insurance) carries a nominal monthly fee for everyone ($11 per month).

(NOTE: THOSE FEW WHO ARE NOT INSURED UNDER SOCIAL SECURITY CAN STILL RECEIVE MEDICARE BY PAYING A MONTHLY PREMIUM.)

IS PART B A GOOD BUY?

Most people do take Part B (medical insurance) along with the free hospital insurance (Part A) they are entitled to because it's a good buy.

The premium, which is currently $11 a month, cannot be more than half the regular cost of protection because the government also pays half. Even if the premium should be increased, you will always get at least twice the value of your money. You may get more.

Considering inflation and the rising cost of medical care, the premium should be much higher than $11, even with a matching $11 paid by the government. But the premium cannot increase by more than the percentage increase in Social Security benefits. This is the law. If Social Security benefits go up by 5 percent, then the premium may also rise by 5 percent. But medical costs are rising much faster than Social Security benefits; so you are receiving high protection at a low rate.

WOULD PRIVATE INSURANCE COST LESS?

Probably not. Medical insurance is very expensive, and climbs right along with medical costs (a much steeper climb than the cost of living). Most of us will pay more visits to the doctor as we grow older. Considering the frequency of these trips to the doctor, plus the low cost of Part B medical insurance, it's likely that you'll be reimbursed for your premium payments (and more) within the year.

You can put off deciding whether or not to take Part B; but the premium goes up 10 per cent for each year you delay (plus any across-the-board increase).

DEPENDENTS

Your husband or wife and other dependents only receive Medicare when they become 65, even if they retire at age 62 and collect Social Security benefits. (Unless they meet the other requirements for people under 65.) Medicare covers individuals; it isn't a family plan. Every person must qualify on his or her own.

IF YOU'RE NOT INSURED BY SOCIAL SECURITY, BUT WANT MEDICARE

* Three months before you reach 65, sign up at your Social Security office.

* There may be special enrollment times if you are over 65 years old. Check with your Social Security office.

* Do not delay. The premium rate increases by 10 per cent for every year you could have received Medicare but didn't.

You will have to pay for both parts of your Medicare insurance. As of July 1981, Part A hospital insurance costs $78 per month; Part B medical insurance costs $11 per month. *And you must take both parts.*

(*NOTE:* Those who are not covered by Medicare can still get help if they are in serious trouble by applying for *Medicaid*. The Medicaid program is state-run to provide medical services to the needy. You do not have to be on welfare to receive help from Medicaid. Nor do you have to be insured by Social Security. Your nearest Medicaid office is listed in the phone book under *Medicaid Information*.)

HOW TO QUALIFY UNDER AGE 65

A few people are eligible for Medicare even though they have not yet reached the age of 65. A disabled worker can receive Medicare if he or she has been receiving disability benefits from Social Security for at least 24 months. These months do not have to be consecutive, however. There are no age restrictions. If the disabled person returns to substantial gainful employment Medicare coverage will continue for three years. However, should the same person become disabled again within five years, he can resume his Medicare protection immediately.

No one else in the disabled person's family can receive Medicare until they qualify on their own.

Disabled widows and widowers between age 50 and 65 are eligible, as are those people age 18 and over who became disabled before age 22 and who receive Social Security benefits.

Anyone insured by Social Security may qualify for Medicare if he or his dependents need maintenance-dialysis treatment or a kidney transplant. This is true if any member of the insured worker's family has chronic kidney failure. As long as the head of the family—man or woman—is insured under Social Security, any member of the family who requires dialysis or transplant for chronic kidney failure can qualify for Medicare.

However, only the person suffering from the kidney ailment receives Medicare. He or she receives full Medicare benefits.

> (*NOTE:* If you receive Social Security disability the Social Security Administration may inform you that you are also eligible for Medicare. But don't count on it. If you think you might be eligible, apply for Medicare at your nearest Social Security office.)

WOMEN AND MEDICARE

A woman aged 65 can be covered by Medicare either on her husband's Social Security record (provided he is age 65 and enrolled in Medicare), or she can collect on her own. But if she is not 65, she must find other coverage, even though her husband may be covered by Medicare. If she is still working she may already have a health plan at work. If she was covered by her husband's previous health plan before he retired, she might be able to have his old policy transferred to herself on an individual basis after he enrolls in Medicare. If none of these options apply, a woman should seek private health insurance plans to carry her over until she reaches age 65 and becomes eligible for Medicare.

Health insurance policies can be expensive. Individual policies usually cost more than group plans, except when you buy reduced coverage. Even so, an individual plan can give you reasonable protection until you are eligible for Medicare.

ENROLLMENT

You are automatically enrolled in Medicare, both Parts A and B, when you apply for Social Security benefits. You should do this at about three months before you turn 65. If you decide you don't want Part B you will have to advise the Social Security office so they will not automatically deduct the premium from your monthly check.

Working past 65? Still sign up for your Social Security benefits, with the stipulation that you don't want to start your Social Security, but you do want Medicare. They will hold back your benefit checks, but you still receive you Medicare card. You can collect all Medicare benefits even though you are not retired.

(IMPORTANT: Apply on time [a few months early is better]. If you are late, your Part A hospital insurance is retroactive for twelve months. But Part B is limited. If you fail to enroll on time, and subsequently try to collect, you may find that you were not covered.)

IF YOU WORK FOR THE GOVERNMENT

Government employees usually have their own health plans that provide coverage similar to that offered by Medicare. In some instances government employees can adjust their Federal health plans to combine with Medicare and get a broader, even more comprehensive insurance package.

PERMANENT KIDNEY FAILURE: SPECIAL RULES

Medicare health insurance is available to most people who have permanent kidney failure and need regular kidney dialysis treatments or a kidney transplant.

Regardless of your age, if you need maintenance dialysis or transplant surgery because of permanent kidney failure, you are eligible for Medicare if:

1. You have worked long enough to be insured under Social Security or the Railroad Retirement system; or

2. You are already getting monthly Social Security or railroad retirement benefits; or

3. You are the spouse or dependent child of someone insured or getting benefits under Social Security or the railroad retirement system.

Only the family member who has permanent kidney failure is eligible for Medicare protection.

How to Apply

As soon as you know that you need maintenance dialysis treatments or kidney transplant surgery, you should apply for Medicare at any Social Security office. The people there will help you obtain any evidence you need. If you can't come to the office, a representative can visit you to take an application.

Costs to You

Medicare has two parts—hospital insurance and medical insurance. If you are eligible, hospital insurance is free. You pay a monthly premium for medical insurance. You are not required to take medical insurance if you don't want to, but many services for the treatment of permanent kidney failure are covered *only* under Part B medical insurance.

Other Services

People eligible for Medicare because of permanent kidney failure receive *all Medicare benefits*. You have the same Medicare protection as people who qualify because they are 65 or older. So in addition to the care you need for permanent kidney failure, Medicare can help pay for many other hospital and medical services.

What's Covered

Medicare hospital insurance (Part A) helps pay for kidney transplant surgery and related inpatient hospital services.

Medicare medical insurance (Part B) covers outpatient maintenance dialysis. Part B also helps pay for doctors' services, including surgeons' services for transplant surgery; outpatient self-dialysis training; and home dialysis equipment, supplies, and periodic support services.

Approved Facilities

To receive Medicare payments, medical facilities must be specifically approved to provide maintenance dialysis, self-dialysis training, or kidney transplant surgery. These facilities do not necessarily have to participate in other Medicare health care services to qualify.

Approved facilities must meet special health, safety, professional, staffing, and minimum utilization standards that are directly related to dialysis and kidney transplant services. They also must meet Federal, state, and local requirements for medical facility planning. The medical facility can tell you whether it is approved by Medicare for payment of dialysis and transplant services. Or, your doctor may know.

How Soon Does Coverage Begin?

If you are receiving maintenance dialysis treatments, your Medicare protection starts on the first day of the third month after the month you begin treatments. For example, if you begin receiving maintenance dialysis treatments in May, your Medicare coverage would begin on August 1st.

There are two ways Medicare coverage can begin earlier:

* Benefits can begin in the first month of dialysis if you join in a self-dialysis training program in an approved facility before the third month of dialysis begins, *and* you are expected to complete the training and self-dialyze thereafter.

* Benefits can begin the month you are admitted to a hospital for kidney transplant or preliminary procedures if the transplant takes place in that month or within the two following months.

How Long Does Coverage Last?

Medicare coverage ends 12 months after the month you no longer require maintenance dialysis treatments or 36 months following a kidney transplant. (Unless you are eligible for Medicare on another basis besides permanent kidney failure.)

If the transplant fails during or after that 36-month period so that you again need maintenance dialysis or another transplant, Medicare coverage will continue or be reinstated immediately without any new waiting period.

Your Medicare Part B medical insurance coverage, however, can stop before that for failure to pay premiums or if you decide to cancel this part of your Medicare protection.

Additional Help

If you have health care protection from another source — for example, from private health insurance, the VA, the Indian Health Service, or a Federal employees' health plan — it may help pay for your treatment.

There are also agencies in most states that can help with some of the medical expenses Medicare does not cover. Some states have Kidney Commissions that help people who need assistance in meeting expenses of kidney dialysis and transplant services. And most states have a Medicaid program that helps pay medical expenses in case of serious financial need.

MEDICARE AND WORKMEN'S COMPENSATION

If you are still working past age 65 and are injured on the job, you may be covered by Workmen's Compensation. It depends on the state you live in, and the nature of the job. If you do receive money from Workmen's Compensation to pay for your medical bills, Medicare will not contribute. But if Workmen's Compensation pays only part of the medical costs, Medicare will usually pick up the rest (providing of course that you are enrolled in Medicare).

DO YOU PAY TAXES ON MEDICARE BENEFITS?

Any money or benefits you receive from Medicare is not taxable. You do not even report the money Medicare contributes on your income tax. However, any money you pay out towards premiums, deductibles or your share of medical bills can be *deducted* from your taxes. Be sure to claim these expenses under "medical deductions" on your income tax statement.

QUESTIONS AND ANSWERS: GENERAL

Question: What is Medicare?

Answer: Medicare is a health-insurance program set up under Social Security to help Americans 65 years old or older, as well as severly disabled people under 65, in paying for health care. It has two parts—hospital insurance, known as Part A of Medicare, and medical insurance, known as Part B of Medicare. Hospital insurance helps pay for services you receive as a patient in a hospital or skilled nursing facility and for certain follow-up services you receive after leaving the hospital or nursing facility. Medical insurance helps pay for physicians' services, outpatient hospital services and other medical items and services not covered by hospital insurance. People enrolled in medical insurance pay monthly premium of $9.60 during the 12 month period beginning July 1980. As of July 1981, the premium will increase to $11 per month.

Question: Who is eligible for Medicare?

Answer: Nearly everyone over the age of 65 is eligible. So are disabled people who have been getting Social Security disability benefits for two years or more, and people insured under Social Security who need dialysis treatment or a kidney transplant because of chronic kidney disease. In addition, spouses or children of insured people may be eligible if they need kidney dialysis or transplant.

Question: Am I still eligible for Medicare if I reach 65 but decide not to retire?

Answer: Yes. But you should tell your Social Security office two or three months before you become 65.

Question: I know there are things hospital insurance won't cover, and things medical insurance won't cover. Are there any things that neither will cover?

Answer: Yes, services that are neither reasonable nor necessary for the diagnosis or treatment of an injury or illness; cosmetic surgery, except when done in connection with the prompt repair of an accidental injury or for the improvement of a malformed body member; services that neither the patient nor another party on his behalf has a legal obligation to pay for, such as a free chest X-ray; certain services payable through other Federal, state or local programs, and services furnished by immediate relatives, or members of the patient's household, eyeglasses, hearing aids, homemaker services, routine physical examination and tests.

Question: What people are affected by the new rule making Medicare available to the disabled who aren't 65 years old yet?

Answer: In addition to all disabled workers who have been receiving Social Security or railroad-retirement disability benefits for two years or more, Medicare coverage has been extended to disabled workers of any age, disabled widows and widowers who are 50 to 65 years old; mothers 50 years old or older who became disabled in the last two years but did not seek disability payments because they were collecting benefits as the mothers of young or disabled children in their care; and people disabled before age 22 providing they have been receiving disability benefits for two years or more.

Question: Where does the Medicare program get the money for the benefits it pays?

Answer: Briefly, the money for Part A of the program, or hospital insurance, comes from contributions made by employees, their employers and self-employed people. The money for Part B, or medical insurance, comes from the monthly premiums paid by people who are enrolled, and from the Federal government, which by laws pays at least half.

Question: Does any organization check up on the Medicare program to make sure it's not wasteful?

Answer: Yes. Professional Standards Review Organizations, made up of physicians, have been set up to monitor Medicare.

Question: Do most health facilities take part in the program?

Answer: Yes. To do so, they must meet certain standards of care, they must not charge you for services that Medicare is supposed to pay for, and they must avoid discrimination based on race, color or national origin.

Question: How can I prove to the hospital that I've got both hospital and medical insurance?

Answer: People who have Medicare's hospital insurance or medical insurance—or both—are given a health-insurance card. Show it to the staff at the hospital, at the physician's office, or wherever you receive services. The card tells your name, sex and claim number, and also shows what insurance you have and when it became effective. If a wife and husband both have Medicare, they are issued separate cards and claim numbers.

Question: I've lost my health-insurance card. Now what?

Answer: Your Social Security office will get you a new one.

Question: How can I find out if a hospital participates in Medicare?

Answer: Ask your physician, your Social Security office or someone at the hospital.

Question: When I became 65 years old, I didn't qualify for Medicare hospital coverage because I didn't have enough of a work record under Social Security. Is there some other way I can get hospital insurance? I'm not disabled.

Answer: You can get the hospital insurance by paying a premium of $78 a month. However, you will have to enroll in medical insurance also.

Question: I'm trying to see the world, but not at the risk of forgoing Medicare. Will I be covered outside the United States?

Answer: Payments usually are made only for services in the 50 states, the District of Columbia, Puerto Rico, the Virgin

Islands, American Samoa and Guam. However, hospital insurance will pay for services you receive in foreign hospitals under certain conditions, generally if the foreign hospital is closer to you than is the nearest United States hospital that can give the care you need.

Question: My kidneys are bad and I've been on dialysis treatment for a month. Is that long enough to qualify for Medicare?

Answer: You're half way there. You have to be on dialysis for at least two months before Medicare can help you. However, there are ways coverage can begin sooner. Check with your Social Security office.

Question: Can I get my kidney dialysis treatment or—if it comes to that—my kidney transplant, at any hospital, and still be covered by Medicare?

Answer: You are limited to those medical facilities specifically approved to provide maintenance dialysis or kidney transplant surgery. Your doctor or the facility can tell you whether a facility is approved by Medicare for payment of dialysis and transplant services.

Question: How much will Medicare pay for kidney treatments?

Answer: The program will pay 80 per cent of the reasonable charges.

Question: I'm hoping to use a dialysis machine at home so I won't have to spend all that time in a hospital. Can I still get aid from Medicare?

Answer: Yes. The program will pay 80 per cent of the training costs, 80 per cent of the price of the machine (or, if you decide to rent one, 80 per cent of the rental fee), and 80 per cent of the cost for necessary chemicals and filters. Medical insurance can cover the services of a trained dialysis aide to assist with self-dialysis at home if certain conditions are met. Check with your Social Security office.

MEDICARE: PART A

HOSPITAL INSURANCE

As you know, Medicare coverage is divided into two parts. Part A—hospital insurance—is available without charge to all those eligible for Social Security. Part B is medical insurance for which a small monthly premium is charged. As soon as you sign up for Social Security you are automatically enrolled in both parts of Medicare when you turn 65. But you do not have to take Part B if you don't want it. Notify the Social Security office so that the Part B premium is not deducted from your Social Security benefits checks.

Part A of Medicare is designed exclusively to pay for hospitalization. It is free automatically to anyone 65 or older who is eligible for Social Security. If you are one of the few people not insured by Social Security you are probably still eligible for Medicare when you reach 65 (there are very few exceptions), but you will have to pay a monthly premium of $78 for Part A (plus $11 for Part B).

In addition to hospital bills, Part A also pays for treatment in a skilled nursing facility after you leave the hospital, and/or skilled care in your home. Even though Part A is free to most eligible people you pay no monthly premium, a standard deductible must be met before Part A goes into effect.

Whether you stay in the hospital one day or three months, you must first pay $204 before Part A hospital insurance takes over.

This deductible must be met for each new benefit period. A benefit period is 90 days. After you pay $204, Medicare will pay all your hospital bills for the next 60 days. If you are still in the hospital, you will have to pay $51 for each additional day for the next 30 days. After that, the benefit period runs out.

If you are still hospitalized after the 90-day benefit period is up, you will have to assume all the costs of hospitalization yourself. However, everyone in Medicare has a lifetime reserve fund that amounts to 60 days of hospital care. You can use these reserve days anytime you wish. But once you have used them, they are gone. Reserve days are not renewable in the same way that benefits periods are. If you have to dip into your lifetime reserve days you will have to pay $102 of the hospital cost for each day you use.

Here's a capsule of Part A hospital coverage:

Medical Service Covered	You Pay
Hospitalization:	
Day 1 through 60	$240 for first 60 days
Day 61 through 90	$51/day
Lifetime reserve: 60 days	$102/day
Skilled Nursing Facility: 100 days/each benefit	Free for 20 days. After 20 days, you pay $25.50 each day
Skilled Home Health Care 100 visits	Free

BENEFIT PERIODS

Each benefit period covers 90 days of hospital care. After you pay the $204 deductible, you receive 60 days of hospital care without charge, and 30 additional days for which you pay $51 each day.

There is no limit to the number of benefit periods you may have when you are insured by Medicare. But you must have a 60-

day break between benefit periods. That is, you will have to stay out of the hospital or skilled nursing facility for at least 60 days before a new Medicare benefit period is activated again.

For example, if you go home after 25 days in the hospital and have to be readmitted 30 days later, you do not begin a new benefit period. You still have 65 days left in the same benefit period. (You have used up 25 of your 90 days.)

But if you go home after 25 days in the hospital and stay out of the hospital for 60 days before you are readmitted—then you would start a *new* benefit period for which you would be covered for 90 more days.

WHAT'S COVERED BY PART A

When Part A is in effect, you are entitled to:

* A semi-private room (two to four beds in a room)
* Operating and recovery room charges
* Services in intensive care
* Regular nursing service
* All meals, including special diets
* Drugs (supplied and administered by the hospital)
* Laboratory tests, X-rays, and other radiological services
* Medical supplies such as surgical dressings, casts, etc.
* Use of appliances and equipment furnished by hospital or skilled nursing facility
* Inpatient rehabilitation services

WHAT'S NOT COVERED BY PART A

There are several important—and expensive—items that Part A does not cover. These include:

* Physicians' and surgeons' bills (these will be covered if you also have Part B medical insurance)

* Private duty nurses

* Any extra charges for a private room (unless required for medical reasons)

* The first three pints of blood you need in a benefit period

* Personal comfort or convenience items such as charges for telephone, television, or radio

SKILLED NURSING FACILITIES

A skilled nursing facility is a nursing home that provides skilled care or rehabilitation services under the direction of a doctor. Rehabilitation centers would also come under the general heading of "skilled nursing facility." You will be covered under Medicare Part A if you enter a skilled nursing facility after a hospital stay of at least three days. Your doctor must order the transfer and the Medicare review board must approve. Medicare will help pay the bill only if you are sent to a skilled nursing facility for actual *treatment*.

This means that if you need general care while you recover from an illness or an operation—even if you are in a skilled nursing facility—Medicare does not pay. Your need for custodial care may be perfectly legitimate; you may need help changing dressings, preparing or eating food, walking or dressing—but Medicare cannot help.

To receive Medicare you must require *skilled* nursing or rehabilitation treatment every day. Rehabilitation services include physical, occupational, and speech therapy. Medicare Part A will help pay the cost of skilled services, and also covers the cost of the following:

* Semi-private room (two to four beds in a room)

* All meals, including special diets

* Regular nursing service

* Rehabilitation services

* Medical supplies such as splints and casts

* Drugs supplied by the skilled nursing facility
* Medical social services
* Use of appliances and equipment such as braces or a wheelchair

Medicare will NOT cover the cost of:

* Physicians' services

    Private duty nurses

* Any extra charge for a private room (unless required for medical reasons)
* Personal comfort or convenience items such as radio, television, or telephone at your request

How Much Does Medicare Pay?

If you are moved to a skilled nursing facility (usually within 14 days of your hospital stay) your benefit period is 100 days. For the first 20 days, Medicare picks up all the tabs. For the next 80 days, you have to share in the expenses by paying $25.50 a day.

HOME HEALTH CARE

Home health care coverage is provided to help pay for skilled treatment that you otherwise would receive in a skilled nursing facility. Usually, if you need only part-time treatment you can receive assistance at home. But again, Medicare helps only when you require *skilled* treatment by trained personnel. If you need someone to come in to help you dress or eat or clean your house, Medicare does not pay, even though these needs are specific and legitimate. Nor will Medicare provide full-time nursing care at home, or pay for any drugs or other medications you may need.

Hospital insurance does not pay for things that people without professional training could do for you. However, Medicare will pay for medical supplies and appliances that are required for your treatments. Trained practitioners include speech therapists, physical or occupational therapists, and skilled nurses.

MEDICARE (PART A)

To receive home health care visits you must have been in a hospital for at least three days. You are entitled to a maximum of 100 home visits in any 12-month period following release from a hospital or skilled nursing facility. Home health visits must be provided by an agency participating in Medicare.

SOME EXTRA BENEFITS UNDER PART A

Hospital insurance also includes limited care in a psychiatric hospital (up to 190 days in a lifetime). In an emergency, you will receive care in the nearest hospital, even if it is not a participant in the Medicare program. And you may also receive care in a Christian Science sanatorium if it is certified by the First Church of Christ, Scientist, in Boston.

QUESTIONS AND ANSWERS: PART A

Question: What services will hospital insurance pay for?

Answer: When you are an inpatient of a hospital or a skilled nursing facility, hospital insurance covers the cost of room and meals, including special diets, in a semi-private room (two to four beds); regular nursing services, services in an intensive-care unit of a hospital, drugs, supplies, appliances and equipment furnished by the hospital or skilled nursing facility; medical social services, laboratory tests, operating-room charges and X-ray and other radiology services.

Question: What services are not included under hospital insurance?

Answer: Hospital insurance does not pay for physicians' bills (although these will be covered if you also have medical insurance), private-duty nurses, personal-comfort or convenience items such as charges for a telephone, a radio or a television set provided at your request; any extra charges for the use of a private room, unless you need a private room for medical reasons; the first three pints of blood you need during a "benefit period" while you are an inpatient in a hospital or skilled nursing facility, and any care you may get in a hospital or skilled nursing facility when the main reason for your admission or stay is your need for help with such activities as bathing, eating, dressing, walking, or taking medicine at the right time—things that you'd ordinarily do for yourself or that can be done for you by people without professional training.

Question: How much of my expenses will hospital insurance pay?

Answer: When you are a hospital bed patient because only a hospital can provide the care you need, hospital insurance will pay for up to 90 days in each "benefit period" if you are in a participating general-care, tuberculosis or psychiatric hospital. For the first 60 days, all covered services will be paid for, except for the first $204 worth. For the 61st through the 90th day, all covered services, except for $51 a day will be paid for.

When you are a bed patient in a skilled nursing facility, hospital insurance will pay for up to 100 days in each "benefit period" if you are in a participating facility. For the first 20 days, all covered services will be paid for. For the 21st day through the 100th day, all covered services, except for $25.50 per day will be paid for.

When you are a patient receiving home health services, hospital insurance will pay all covered services for up to 100 home health visits in each "benefit period" if the visits are medically necessary and are furnished by a participating home health agency.

Question: What is a benefit period?

Answer: A benefit period is a stretch of time that begins the first time you enter a hospital after your hospital insurance starts, and ends as soon as you have been out of the hospital (or any facility primarily offering skilled nursing care) for 60 consecutive days. Let's say you entered a hospital on Aug. 22 and were released on Aug. 31. Your benefit period started the day you entered, Aug. 22, and will end 60 days after Aug. 31—which would be Oct. 30—provided you don't re-enter the hospital as a bed patient at any time during those 60 days. A new benefit period will then begin the next time you enter a hospital after Oct. 30.

Question: Is there any limit on the number of benefit periods I can have?

Answer: No. However, there is a limit on the amount of benefits you can receive in any one benefit period (see two preceding questions).

Question: What if I can't keep track of the "days" and "visits" I've used up in a benefit period?

Answer: You don't even need to keep track. Whenever you use any hospital-insurance benefits, the Social Security Administration will send you a notice indicating how many "days" and "visits" you have left in your current benefit period.

Question: What happens if I need more than 90 days of hospital care in one benefit period?

Answer: Few people need so much hospitalization that they use up their 90 days. But if you turn out to be one of those people, you will have a "lifetime reserve" of 60 days to draw from. Every time you use a "lifetime reserve" day, hospital insurance will pay for all covered services except for $102 a day. If you need hospital care after your regular 90 days are used up, the extra days will be subtracted automatically from your lifetime reserve.

Question: What if I use up my regular 90 days in a benefit period, but don't want to start using my lifetime reserve? I'm thinking that maybe the private insurance I carry will pay for some or all of the extra days I need.

Answer: Notify your hospital in writing. You might also ask your physician or the hospital staff to help you decide whether to draw on your lifetime reserve.

Question: If I use up my benefit days in a given benefit period, can my medical insurance take over and pay for what my hospital insurance will no longer cover?

Answer: For some services, yes. The services include diagnostic laboratory tests done by approved independent laboratories, radiation therapy and diagnostic X-rays, portable diagnostic X-rays done in your home under a physician's supervision, surgical dressings and devices, the rental or purchase of durable medical equipment—such as crutches or a wheelchair—prescribed by a physician for use in your home, certain ambulance services, and devices, other than dental devices, to replace all or part of an internal organ.

Question: What do I have to do to get hospital insurance?

Answer: Everyone who is 65 years old or more and is entitled to monthly Social Security or railroad-retirement benefits gets hospital insurance automatically without paying monthly premiums. If you are receiving monthly Social Security checks, you will be contacted by mail a few months before you become 65. If you are disabled and have been getting Social Security disability benefits for two years or more, you will also get hospital insurance automatically.

Question: I am 65 but haven't stopped working (I refuse to retire!). Can I still get hospital insurance?

Answer: Yes, if you have worked long enough at jobs covered by Social Security or by the railroad-retirement plan. If you became 65 years old in 1973, you need 18 quarters of coverage. If you became 65 years old in 1974 you need 21 quarters of coverage. For men who became 65 in 1975 or later and women who attained 65 in 1974 or later the same quarters of coverage necessary for retirement benefits are required for hospital insurance protection.

Question: What about people like me who are 65 or older but are not automatically entitled to hospital insurance?

Answer: You can buy hospital insurance for a monthly premium of $78, but will also have to enroll for medical insurance.

Question: I'm not sure whether or not I'm eligible for hospital insurance. How can I find out?

Answer: Contact your Social Security office two or three months before you reach 65.

Question: As a disabled railroad worker, can I get hospital insurance?

Answer: Yes, but there are special requirements. You and others who receive railroad disability annuities or retirement benefits because of a disability should contact a railroad-retirement office.

Question: I'm a disabled widow, not yet 65 years old, with two children. Am I entitled to hospital insurance?

Answer: If you are at least 50 years old and have been severely disabled at least two years, but haven't filed a claim

MEDICARE (PART A)

based on your disability because you were getting Social Security checks as a mother with your children, you should contact your Social Security office. Yes, you might be eligible for hospital insurance.

Question: Where does the hospital-insurance program get the money to pay for all the benefits and services?

Answer: The hospital-insurance program, like the Social Security program, gets its money from contributions made by employees, their employers, and self-employed people. For 1981, the contribution rate is 1.30% of $29,700 in wages and/or 1.30% of $29,700 in self-employment income. Money also comes from the premiums paid by people who want hospital insurance but are not automatically entitled to it. The contributions and premiums go into the Hospital Insurance Trust Fund, from which the benefits and administrative expenses are paid. Money from general tax revenues is used to pay benefits for people who are insured under a special provision in the initial law even though they are not entitled to Social Security or railroad-retirement benefits.

Question: Are any studies done to make sure the payment levels are kept up to date?

Answer: Yes. By law, the various dollar amounts for which you as a patient would be responsible are reviewed every year. If the review shows that hospital costs have changed significantly, the amounts must be adjusted for the next year.

Question: The hospital where I received emergency care does not participate in Medicare. Can I still get hospital insurance to help pay the bill?

Answer: Yes, if the hospital meets certain conditions, if it was the closest, or the closest that had a bed available, and if it was equipped to handle the emergency. The benefit payment will usually be paid to the hospital. However, if the hospital bills you instead of Medicare, the payment will be made to you. Your Social Security office can help you submit the claim.

Question: Does hospital insurance cover any outpatient services?

Answer: No. These are covered only by medical insurance.

Question: Do I have to do anything special on entering the hospial (other than saying I need help)?

Answer: You will be asked to show your health insurance card, sign some forms and give information—or Medicare notices—about any recent stays in a hospital or in a skilled nursing facility. You may be asked to make arrangement for charges not covered by Medicare. Remember that the hospital cannot collect from you for any services your hospital insurance will pay for. If the hospital erroneously collects from you, you will get a refund.

Question: Can benefits be paid if I have to go to a mental hospital?

Answer: Yes, but there is a lifetime limit of 190 hospital-benefit days. And if you are a patient in a psychiatric hospital on the day your hospital insurance starts, the days you have spent in the psychiatric hospital during the preceding 150 days will count against the number of benefit days you can use in the psychiatric hospital in your first benefit period. But these days will not count against your 190-day lifetime maximum.

Question: What is a skilled nursing facility?

Answer: The Social Security Administration defines a skilled nursing facility as a specially qualified facility staffed and equipped to furnish skilled nursing care or skilled rehabilitation services and related health services.

Question: When might I need a skilled nursing facility?

Answer: If you as a hospital patient no longer need all the care a hospital provides but still need daily skilled nursing care or skilled rehabilitation services that cannot be furnished at home, your physician may transfer you from the hospital to a skilled nursing facility.

MEDICARE (PART A)

Question: How do I qualify for hospital-insurance benefits if I'm in a skilled nursing facility? Do I just have to show up?

Answer: All of the following must be true—(1) You need daily skilled nursing care or skilled rehabilitation services; (2) a physician says you need such nursing or rehabilitation care and orders it for you; (3) you have been in a participating or otherwise qualified hospital for at least three consecutive days; (4) you are admitted within a limited period, usually within 14 days of leaving the hospital, and (5) you are admitted for further treatment of a condition for which you were treated at the hospital.

Question: I'm in a skilled nursing facility, but I don't need services constantly—I just need to have my dressings changed once or twice a week. Can my hospital insurance pay for this?

Answer: No. Nor can it pay your bills if you are in the skilled nursing facility mainly because you need help in eating, dressing, getting around, taking medicine and so on, even though these services are done by skilled nurses.

Question: I just got out of a skilled nursing facility, but am going to have to go back. Can I do so and get hospital-insurance coverage without having to spend at least three days in a hospital first?

Answer: Yes, if you are readmitted to a skilled nursing facility within 14 days of being released.

Question: What services in a skilled nursing facility are covered by hospital insurance?

Answer: Hospital insurance will help pay for lodging in a semi-private room (two to four beds), all meals, including special diets; regular nursing services; physical, occupational and speech therapy; medical supplies such as splints and casts, drugs furnished by the skilled nursing facility, medical social services and the use of appliances and equipment, such as a wheelchair or braces, furnished by the nursing facility.

Question: What services in a skilled nursing facility will not be paid by my hospital insurance?

Answer: Your hospital insurance does not cover personal-comfort or convenience items such as charges for a telephone, a radio or a television set furnished at your request, private-duty nurses, any extra charge for a private room, unless you need the room for medical reasons; physicians' services, which would be covered by your medical insurance, and any help with eating, getting about and other personal, daily activities that you'd ordinarily do for yourself or that can be done for you by people without professional training.

Question: I'm being released from the hospital, finally, but will still need some care. However, my doctor says I'd be better off getting the care at home through a home health agency, rather than going to a skilled nursing facility. Will I still be eligible for hospital-insurance coverage?

Answer: Yes, if the care you get at home includes part-time skilled nursing or physical or speech therapy, and if the visits made by the nurses and therapists are medically necessary and are provided by a participating home health agency. This provision also applies if you are returning home after being in a skilled nursing home following a hospital stay.

Question: How long can I get care at home and still be covered by my hospital insurance?

Answer: Benefits can be paid for up to one year after your latest discharge from a hospital or skilled nursing facility, but all of the following must be true—(1) you were in a participating or otherwise qualified hospital for at least three consecutive days; (2) the care you need includes part-time skilled nursing care of physical or speech therapy; (3) you are confined to your home; (4) a physician says you need home health care and sets up a home care plan for you within 14 days after you are released from the hospital or nursing facility, and (5) the care is for further treatment of a condition you were treated for as a bed patient in the hospital or as a patient in the nursing facility.

Question: What home health services will my hospital insurance help pay for?

Answer: It will help pay for part-time skilled nursing care and physical or speech therapy. If you need any of those services, your hospital insurance will also cover occupational therapy, medical social services, part-time services from home health aides, and medical supplies and appliances furnished by the home health agency.

Question: What home health services will not be covered by my hospital insurance?

Answer: Hospital insurance does not pay for full-time nursing care, drugs and biologicals, personal-comfort or convenience items, meals delivered to your home and custodial care—that is, any help you get with such personal daily needs as eating and getting about, things that you'd ordinarily do for yourself or that people without professional training could do for you.

Question: Will I be covered by hospital insurance if I'm treated in a foreign hospital?

Answer: Yes, under certain conditions. In emergency cases, if you are in the United States when the emergency occurs and a foreign hospital is closer to you than is the nearest hospital in the United States that could provide the care you need, your hospital insurance will help pay for your emergency care. In non-emergency cases, if a foreign hospital is closer to your home than is the nearest United States hospital that can give the care you need, hospital insurance will help pay for the covered services you receive in a foreign hospital. If you become injured or ill while traveling through Canada, to or from Alaska and another state, hospital insurance can cover inpatient hospital care in a Canadian hospital.

Question: I've been getting treatment in a Christian Science sanitorium. Is this covered by my hospital insurance?

Answer: Yes. Hospital insurance can help pay for certain hospital and extended-care services provided to inpatients of a sanitorium operated, listed or certified by the First Church of Christ, Scientist, in Boston.

Question: Can Medicare payments to my hospital or skilled nursing facility be stopped for any reason?

Answer: Yes, if the hospital or nursing facility's watchdog body, known as a Utilization Review Committee, decides that the care you're receiving is not medically necessary. These committees, which are active at each hospital and skilled nursing facility, seek to assure the most effective use of the services furnished. Each committee includes at least two physicians and reviews all long stay cases. Admissions are reviewed on a sample basis. The committee always discusses its findings with a patient's physician when it decides that the care the patient is receiving is medically unnecessary and that the payments must be stopped. If the committee stays with its decision, the patient, his physician and the hospital or nursing facility are told in writing. The payments must then stop within three days after the facility has received notice. The Utilization Review Committees decide whether the care you're receiving is medically necessary, not whether the care is covered by hospital insurance. The latter decision is made by intermediaries selected by the Federal government.

Question: I strongly suspect my hospital-insurance payments are incorrect. What should I do?

Answer: Contact whoever supplied your services. If they can't help, they will refer you to the organization that handles their Medicare payments. If you're still unsatisfied, your Social Security office can inform you about your right to appeal.

MEDICARE: PART B

MEDICAL INSURANCE

Part B of Medicare is *medical* insurance. For a nominal monthly premium, Part B helps pay physicians' and surgeons' bills. This includes visits to your regular doctor in his office. And also includes all physician's bills if you are in a hospital. Doctors' bills — including surgeons' and anesthesiologists' — are not covered by Part A.

Part B also helps pay for any hospital service you need if you are not actually *in* the hospital. Hospital services you might receive as an outpatient include medical treatment, social medical services, rental or purchase of medical equipment and supplies. If you are sick but don't require hospitalization, Part B will help.

Everyone who takes Part B medical insurance pays a premium (as of July 1981, $11 per month). There is also a $60 deductible that must be met every year. Once the deductible has been paid, Medicare pays 80 percent of reasonable charges, and you pay the remaining 20 percent.

Here's a capsule of Part B medical coverage:

* Treatment in your doctor's office, including services of the doctor's nurse, drugs and biologicals you cannot administer yourself, medical supplies, speech or physical therapy, and X-rays associated with your treatment.

Hospital Services

* Treatment in an emergency room or outpatient clinic
* Outpatient physical and speech therapy services. (*Note:* If you receive treatment in the office of a licensed physical therapist, Medicare will pay only $80 each year.)
* Laboratory tests
* X-rays and other radiology services
* Medical supplies such as splints and casts
* Drugs and other medicines you cannot administer yourself

Home Health Visits

Home health visits under Part B are similar to those provided by Part A hospital insurance. The major difference is that you do not have to have been in the hospital to receive home visits under Part B. But the services are essentially the same: part-time skilled nursing care, including physical therapy and speech therapy, occupational therapy, medical social services, and medical supplies furnished by the home health agency. These visits are provided without cost after the $60 yearly deductible has been met. They are *added to*, not replaced by, home health visits provided under Part A.

Medical Service Covered	You Pay
In the Hospital: Physician's & Surgeon's services	$60 deductible each year
Out of the Hospital: Diagnosis and/or treatment of injury or illness by a physician; and outpatient hospital care	$60 deductible each year; plus 20 per cent of reasonable fee set by Medicare
Home Health Services: 100 visits each year	$60 deductible each year

WHAT'S COVERED BY PART B

Doctor's Services

* Medical and surgical treatment when you are in the hospital (includes bills from radiologists, anesthesiologists, pathologists, etc)
* Diagnosis and treatment in your doctor's office
* Diagnostic tests and procedures connected with your treatment

SOME EXTRA BENEFITS UNDER PART B

* Diagnostic tests performed by independent laboratories (must be Medicare-approved)
* Ambulance transportation, if medically necessary, to nearest appropriate facility. The ambulance must meet Medicare requirements.
* Medical equipment prescribed by your doctor (oxygen tanks, wheelchairs, etc.)
* At-home X-rays if ordered by your doctor
* Prosthetic devices (heart pacemakers, corrective lenses following cataract operation, colostomy bags, etc.)
* Medical supplies ordered by your physician (surgical dressings, casts, etc.)

WHAT'S NOT COVERED BY PART B

* Routine tests
* Routine physical examinations
* Eye exams or eyeglasses
* Hearing exams or hearing aids
* Immunizations (unless there is an immediate risk of infec-

tion or you have sustained an injury that requires immunization such as a tetanus shot)
* Dental care, unless associated with surgery of the jaw
* Routine foot care
* Cosmetic surgery, unless required by accidental injury or to correct a malformed part of the body

SOME SPECIAL CASES

Radiology Treatment. Medicare Part B will pay 100 per cent of reasonable charges in a hospital with no deductible. Part B pays 80 percent of out-patient radiology charges after deductible has been met.

Mental Treatment. Part B will pay up to $250 in one year for out-patient mental therapy.

Chiropractor. Only one service is covered: manual manipulation of the spine to correct a subluxation that is visible on X-ray. The chiropractor must be licensed. (Medicare does not cover the cost of the X-rays taken by the chiropractor.)

Podiatrist. Routine foot care is not covered. Treatment of flat fleet, corns, callouses will not be paid for. But Medicare Part B will pay for foot treatment of a medical condition that affects the lower limbs. What they're thinking of, of course, is diabetes, which often requires regular care by a podiatrist.

Dentist. Regular dental work is not covered. But if you require dental work following surgery of the jaw or setting of fractures of the jaw, it will be paid for by Medicare Part B.

IS PART B WORTH THE MONEY?

Most people over 65 think so. The cost of medical insurance in the United States is extremely high, and getting higher every day. Although the monthly premium you pay for Part B may increase in the future, it cannot outpace the increases in your Social Security cash benefits. That is, if you get a raise in your cash benefits of 5 percent, Medicare is entitled to raise your premium by 5 percent—but no more. And remember, whatever amount you pay for a premium, it is matched by the government. So you are never paying more than half of the actual cost.

It's also important to consider that as you become older you will be requiring more medical services than in the past, and your need for coverage will be greater. (For example, if you require an operation, Part A of Medicare does not cover your surgeon's bill, which may be high.)

Will Union or Company Plans Cover It?

Those who are covered by company or union medical insurance may already have adequate protection. If so, they wouldn't need Part B of Medicare. If you are in a company or union plan, look it over carefully. Compare your plan to the Medicare Part B and see which gives you the best coverage. Also make sure that your company or union plan continues to cover you *after* you retire.

You can put deciding whether or not to take Part B; but the premium goes up 10 per cent for each year you delay (plus any across-the-board increase).

THE MEDICARE SEAL OF APPROVAL

Hospitals, therapists, equipment, and services paid for by Medicare must meet certain requirements. Treatment facilities must be licensed by both the state and local health authoritites. And Medicare may impose further requirements before giving its official approval. Before undergoing any treatment or receiving any medical service—including a ride in an ambulance or a bedside X-ray in your home—ask if it is Medicare approved. If it isn't, you may be incurring an out-of-pocket expense. The only exception might be if you require emergency treatment in a hospital or facility not approved by Medicare.

PAYING YOUR BILLS

After the yearly deductible has been met, Medicare pays 80 per cent of a "reasonable charge." And you pay the remaining 20 per cent. The big question is: What does Medicare consider a "reasonable charge?"

The idea is to create some sort of standard fee system. Your physician is free to set his own rates. But Medicare also sets its own rates. Sometimes, the two don't match, and your physician charges more than Medicare considers reasonable.

IS "REASONABLE CHARGE" REALLY REASONABLE?

The "reasonable charge" is different in various parts of the country. Medicare sets the standard charge by taking an average of medical fees in each area. But the schedule is always at least a year behind because Medicare computes the figures over a year's time, then puts the result into effect on July 1 of the following year.

Doctors are much more likely than Medicare to keep abreast of inflation. While Medicare's reasonable charge may be based on 1980 figures, your doctor's bills are based on 1981.

And it is also true that many doctors charge what the traffic will bear, so that one doctor may charge very high rates for the same service that another charges moderate rates for.

You may not know if your doctor's bill outstrips Medicare's "reasonable charge" until you get the bill. There is only one way to protect yourself.

Medicare will pay your medical bills in one of two ways. You can receive the payment directly; then you pay the doctor personally. Or you can have the payment "assigned" to your physician. Here's the advantage to the assignment method:

Your doctor must agree in advance to a Medicare assignment. If he agrees to the method of payment, he is also agreeing to charge the reasonable fee designated by Medicare. medicare pays him 80 per cent of the reasonable charge directly, and you pay him the other 20 per cent. If you have not yet reached your deductible for the year, Medicare will withhold that amount from the doctor's check and you will have to make it up to him.

Naturally, some doctor's don't like to accept Medicare assignments. But you have a right to ask. Whenever you need a doctor's care, always ask *first* if he or she will take a Medicare assignment.

Be definite, specific, and determined. If he refuses, you have only two choices. You can go out and find yourself another good doctor. Or, if you think you must have the services of that special doctor, you will have to pay the difference yourself. Medicare will not bend the fee schedule.

Again, the rule here is to ask first. Once you have received the treatment it's too late to argue.

QUESTIONS AND ANSWERS: PART B

Question: I know medical insurance doesn't cover everything. Can you tell me what services it does cover?

Answer: Briefly, medical insurance will help pay for physicians' services, outpatient hospital services, home health visits, outpatient physical-therapy and speech-pathology services, certain ambulance services, a certain service by chiropractors, home and office services by independent physical therapists and certain medical and health services and supplies.

Question: And what things are not covered?

Answer: Again briefly, medical insurance does not cover routine physical check-ups, prescription drugs and patient medicines, eyeglasses and examinations to fit glasses, hearing aids, immunizations, dentures and routine dental care, orthopedic shoes, personal-comfort items and the first three pints of blood you receive in a calendar year.

Question: I want medical insurance. How can I get it?

Answer: Most people who first became entitled to hospital insurance in July, 1973, or later, will be enrolled automatically for medical insurance, as will people eligible for Medicare because they are disabled (if they have been receiving disability benefits for 26 months). If you are one of these people, information will be mailed to you three months before you become entitled to hospital insurance. But you don't have to do a thing—you will be covered automatically.

Question: What if I don't want medical insurance?

Answer: The information mailed to you three months before you become entitled to hospital insurance will tell you what to do.

Question: I became entitled to hospital insurance before July 1, 1973. Since I won't be enrolled automatically for medical insurance, how can I get it?

Answer: Just sign up at your Social Security office.

Question: It won't be long before I'm entitled to medical insurance. But I can't decide whether I want it or not. Do I have to make up my mind right away?

Answer: No. You will have a seven-month enrollment period starting three months before the month you become eligible and ending three months after that month.

Question: My seven-month enrollment period ended last week and I finally decided not to take medical insurance. But I think I made a mistake. Can I get a second chance to enroll?

Answer: Yes. You can sign up during a general enrollment period that runs every year from Jan. 1 through March 31. However, your protection won't start until July. As of April 1, 1981, you can enroll at anytime but there is a three-month wait before coverage begins and your premium will be 10 per cent higher for each 12-month period that you could have been enrolled but were not.

Question: Maybe they're right when they say old people are forgetful. My seven-month enrollment period went by and I simply forgot to say whether I wanted medical insurance. Can I still enroll somehow?

Answer: Yes. You can use the yearly general enrollment period described above.

Question: Can I get medical insurance even though I'm no longer living in the United States?

Answer: Yes. But you will not be enrolled automatically. You will have to sign up at a Social Security office.

Question: I enrolled for medical insurance and now I've decided I don't want it. Can I get out of it?

Answer: Yes. You may cancel whenever you want to. Your protection and premiums will stop at the end of the calendar quarter following the quarter in which your written cancellation notice is received by the Social Security Administration. If you cancel, then decide you want to re-enroll, you can do so during any general enrollment period.

Question: My neighbor says I was foolish to cancel my medical insurance. Why would he say that?

Answer: You may not be able to get equal protection elsewhere. Many health-insurance companies do not offer broad coverage for people 65 years old or older, although they do offer extra insurance for those who already have Medicare medical insurance.

Question: How much are the medical insurance premiums going to cost me?

Answer: For the 12-month period starting July 1, 1980 you will be paying $9.60 per month, unless you delayed a long time in enrolling after your first chance or re-enrolled after canceling. In those cases, you will pay 10 percent extra for each year you were eligible but were not enrolled.

Question: How do I pay the premiums?

Answer: Many people don't have to do anything—their premiums are deducted automatically from their Social Security benefits, their railroad-retirement benefits or their Civil Service annuities. If you do not receive any of these monthly checks, you can pay your premiums directly to the Social Security Administration.

Question: I suppose the premiums are going to get higher with the years?

Answer: It's hard to say no. However, your share of the premium can be increased only if there has been a general increase in Social Security cash benefits since the last time the premium was increased. And the increase in your share is limited to the percentage increase in cash benefits.

Question: How are increases in premiums determined?

Answer: Every year the medical insurance program is reviewed to insure that the program remains on a pay-as-you-go basis. Every December, the results of the review are announced. Any change in your share of the premium takes effect for the 12-month period starting the following July. As of July, 1981 the premium will be $11.

Question: How much will medical insurance pay for the services it covers?

Answer: Each year, once your covered medical expenses exceed what is known as the "$60 deductible," medical insurance pays 80 percent of the so-called "reasonable charges" for all covered services you receive for the rest of the year.

Question: Here's the $64,000 question—What is the $60 deductible?

Answer: Medical insurance can make no payment in any year until you have accumulated $60 worth of "reasonable charges" for covered medical services—services medical insurance is allowed to pay for.

Question: What are these "reasonable charges?"

Answer: Physicians' charges vary, not only from area to area, but also within a given area. So the Medicare program does not have a fixed schedule of charges that physicians everywhere must use. Instead, the program requires that a physician's fee for a service—his "reasonable charge"—be no higher than his customary charge to all his patients for that service. Nor can his fee be higher than the fee for that service made in three out of four cases by all physicians in your area.

Question: Who determines whether a physician's fee really is reasonable?

Answer: This is done by an organization, called a carrier, that the Social Security Administration has selected to handle medical-insurance claims in your area. Carriers regularly review each physician's customary fee for each type of service and the range of fees made by all physicians in your area. The carriers then adjust the reasonable charges if this seems necessary. The carriers generally are insurance companies or medical services. For example, the carrier in Maine is the Union Mutual Life Insurance Company, the carrier in Washington State is Washington Physicians' Service and the carrier in American Samoa is the Hawaii Medical Service Association.

Question: My doctor charged me more than what the carrier in my area says is a reasonable charge for the service he performed. Can he do this and still call his fees a "reasonable charge?"

Answer: In some cases, yes. For example, your physician may have increased his fees recently, and they may not have been in effect long enough for Medicare records to show that they are being charged to all of his patients. Medicare is like many other health-insurance programs in that it does not recognize a higher fee until it is in effect long enough to be considered customary. However, you may have received a higher fee because your physician's charge for the service is in the upper bracket of physicians' charges in your area. In that case, the charge would not be reasonable.

Question: I'm so disorganized—Is there an easy way to keep track of my medical expenses so I'll know when I've met the $60 deductible?

Answer: It's all done for you. Whenever a medical-insurance claim is filed, you will receive a statement indicating how much of your expenses have been credited to the deductible. If you exceed the deductible, the statement will show the amount of the benefit payment.

Question: What if I don't meet the $60 deductible until the end of the year? When January comes, will I have to start all over to try to meet the deductible for the new year?

Answer: No. There is a special carry-over rule for people like you who would otherwise have to meet the yearly deductible twice during a short period. Any medical expenses you have in the last three months of a year will count for your deductible for the next year. Thus you should save the bills you receive in October, November, and December in case you need them next year—make this one of your New Year's resolutions.

Question: When I go to a hospital for outpatient services, should I mention anything about whether I've met the $60 deductible?

Answer: You should show the hospital staff your most recent explanation-of-benefits statement (the statement you receive whenever a medical-insurance claim is filed). It will tell the staff how much of the deductible you have met and how much of it, if any, they can charge you.

Question: I enrolled in medical insurance but also belong to a group health plan. Will there be any conflict between the two? And how will claims and payments be handled?

Answer: Most group health plans—known as group practice prepayment plans because the members pay their premiums in advance—have arranged with the Social Security Administration to get direct payments for any covered services they give to members who are also enrolled in medical insurance. If your group plan has made such an arrangement, you need to make a claim ONLY for covered services you get that are not provided by your plan. Group plans have also arranged to count your membership premiums or your use of plan services toward your $60 deductible. Arrangements vary, of course, so you should recheck the provisions of the plan you have.

Question: What kind of physicians' services will medical insurance help pay for?

Answer: Medical insurance will help pay for medical and surgical services by a doctor of medicine or a doctor of osteopathy; certain medical and surgical services by a doctor of dental medicine or a doctor of dental surgery; certain services by podiatrists that they are authorized to perform by the state in which they practice; services ordinarily performed in a physician's office and included in his bill (such as diagnostic tests and procedures, medical supplies, drugs and biologicals that cannot be self-administered and services done by the physician's office nurse) and limited services by chiropractors.

Question: What physicians' services are not covered by medical insurance?

Answer: Medical insurance does not pay for routine physical checkups, routine foot care and treatment of flat feet and partial dislocations of the feet, eye refractions and examinations for prescribing, fitting and changing eyeglasses; hearing examinations for prescribing, fitting or changing hearing aids; immunizations, unless directly related to an injury or an immediate risk of infection, and services of certain other practitioners, such as naturopaths or Christian Science practitioners.

Question: Can I choose my own doctor?

Answer: Yes.

Question: You said medical insurance also covered outpatient hospital services. What are these?

Answer: They are any services you receive when you go to a hospital for diagnosis or for treatment but are not admitted as a bed patient.

Question: What outpatient services will medical insurance help pay for?

Answer: Medical insurance will help pay for laboratory work, X-ray and other radiology services, services done in an emergency room or in an outpatient clinic, medical supplies such as splints and casts, and other diagnostic services.

Question: What outpatient hospital services are not covered by medical insurance?

Answer: Medical insurance does not cover tests given as part of a routine check-up, eye refractions and examinations for prescribing, fitting or changing eyeglasses; immunizations, unless directly related to an injury or an immediate risk of infection; and hearing examinations for prescribing, fitting or changing hearing aids.

Question: How are the payments for outpatient services made?

Answer: Once you have met your $60 deductible, medical insurance will pay for 80 percent of the reasonable charges for all covered outpatient hospital services you receive. The hospital will apply for the payment and will charge you for any part of the deductible you have not met, plus 20 percent of the remaining reasonable charges. If the fee is $60 or less and the hospital can't determine how much of the deductible you have met, it may charge you the entire bill. If you pay it, any Medicare payments owed to you will be paid to you directly.

Question: Will the hospital take care of making the medical-insurance claim?

Answer: Yes, except in unusual circumstances. If you ever need help with a claim, contact your Social Security office.

Question: Are all outpatient physical-therapy and speech-pathology services covered?

Answer: They are covered if they are furnished under the direct and personal supervision of a physician, or if they are furnished as part of covered home health services, or if they are furnished by a qualified hospital, skilled nursing facility, home health agency, clinic, rehabilitation agency or public health agency and are furnished under a plan set up and periodically reviewed by a physician. Medical insurance will also cover any physical therapy you need if you are a bed patient in a hospital or skilled nursing facility and the therapy cannot be covered by hospital insurance.

Question: How much will medical insurance pay for physical-therapy and speech-pathology services?

Answer: With one exception, the same as for most other covered services—80 percent of all reasonable charges above your $60 deductible. The exception is this: If you received covered services from a licensed physical therapist in his office or in your home, the most that Medicare can pay in one year is $80.

Question: Is any dental work covered?

Answer: Yes, but only dental work involving surgery of the jaw or of related structures or the setting of fractures of the jaw or of facial bones.

Question: Will medical insurance pay for emergency outpatient care I receive at a hospital that doesn't participate in Medicare?

Answer: Yes, if the hospital meets certain conditions. The hospital usually will bill Medicare for the Medicare portion of the charges, and will bill you for any of the $60 deductible you have not met, plus 20 percent of the remaining reasonable charges. Or, the hospital may bill you for the entire amount. In this case, medical insurance will pay you 80 percent of the reasonable charges above the $60 deductible.

Question: I'm told that under my hospital insurance in Part A of Medicare, I can't receive any home health visits unless I've been in a hospital at least three days in a row. But someone said the rules under medical insurance are different. Is that so?

Answer: Yes. Medical insurance will help pay for up to 100 home health visits each year with no hospitalization requirement.

Question: But are there other conditions I have to meet to get these visits?

Answer: Yes. Medical insurance will pay only if all of the following are true: (1) You need part-time skilled nursing care or physical-therapy or speech-therapy services; (2) you are confined to your home; (3) a physician says you need home health care; (4) a physician sets up and periodically reviews the plan for your home health care; and (5) the home health agency is participating in Medicare.

Question: What constitutes a home health visit?

Answer: You have received one "visit" every time you receive a covered health-care service from a home health agency. If you receive two services on the same day (let's say a speech therapist visits you in the morning and a nurse visits you in the afternoon), you have received two "visits." If you receive one service twice in a day (maybe the physical therapist makes two calls) you have also received two "visits."

Question: I don't live in a house as such, but in a home for the elderly. Can I still get "home" health visits?

Answer: Yes. A home for the aged or a similar residential facility can be considered your home for Medicare purposes. However, a nursing home or other place that mainly provides skilled nursing care cannot.

Question: What home health services will medical insurance help pay for?

Answer: Medical insurance will help pay for part-time nursing care, physical therapy and speech therapy. Should you need any of these, the program will also cover occupational therapy, part-time services from home health aides, medical social services and medical supplies and appliances furnished by the home health agency.

Question: What home health services are not included in medical insurance?

Answer: Medical insurance does not cover full-time nursing care, drugs and biologicals, personal-comfort or convenience items, meals delivered to your home and noncovered levels of care. "Noncovered levels of care" is a term used for the custodial care primarily concerned with helping you with your personal daily needs, such as eating and getting about—things that you ordinarily do for yourself, or that can be done for you by people without professional training.

Question: How is the payment claim for home health services taken care of?

Answer: The home health agency will always make the claim. Medical insurance pays 100 percent, rather than 80 percent, of the reasonable charges above the $60 deductible. So the agency will bill you only for any part of the deductible you haven't met.

Question: What if I use an ambulance? Will medical insurance pay for it?

Answer: Yes, under certain conditions. Medical insurance will help pay for transportation by an approved ambulance service to a hospital or skilled nursing facility only if the ambulance, its equipment and personnel meet Medicare requirements, and if transportation by other means could endanger the patient's health. If you are taken to a facility that is not the nearest one that can provide the care you need, only the reasonable charge for the ambulance transportation to the nearest facility will be covered. With similar restrictions, medical insurance will cover ambulance transportation from one hospital to another, from a hospital to a skilled nursing facility to the patient's home.

Question: What types of miscellaneous medical services and supplies are covered by medical insurance?

Answer: Your medical insurance also covers a range of items you may need because of illness or injury. All can be provided in connection with treatment by your physician, by a medical clinic or by some other health facility. These items include diagnostic laboratory tests done by approved independent laboratories, radiation therapy and diagnostic X-rays, portable diagnostic X-rays done in your home under a physician's supervision, surgical dressings and devices, the rental or purchase of durable medical equipment—such as crutches or a wheelchair—prescribed by a physician for use in your home, certain ambulance services and devices, other than dental devices, to replace all or part of an internal organ. These devices include corrective lenses after a cataract operation.

Question: How about hearing aids, eyeglasses, and false teeth? Are these covered?

Answer: No. Nor are prescription drugs and drugs, such as insulin, that you can administer yourself. Orthopedic shoes or other supportive footwear are not covered by medical insurance unless the shoes are part of leg braces.

Question: How are payment claims for these miscellaneous services and supplies made?

Answer: The participating hospital, skilled nursing facility or home health agency that provides the services for you will

MEDICARE (PART B)

make the claim and will bill you for any of the $60 deductible you have not met, plus 20 percent of the remaining reasonable charges. In other cases, you or whoever supplies the services will make the claim.

Question: If I decide to rent instead of buy the durable medical equipment I need, will medical insurance keep on paying as long as I'm still renting?

Answer: The payments stop when your need for the equipment ends. The same is true if you buy the equipment. The payments are made over a period of time and are based on the reasonable rental rate for the equipment you have.

Question: Does medical insurance cover doctor's services I get for mental illness?

Answer: Yes, but the payments are limited to $250 in a year, when these services are furnished outside the hospital.

Question: Is it true there are special rules regarding the payment for radiology or pathology services?

Answer: If you are an inpatient in a participating hospital and receive these services, medical insurance pays the full reasonable charges made by the physicians. Because the charges are fully paid, they do not count toward your $60 deductible.

Question: I received radiology treatment but received the doctor bills anyway. Now what do I do?

Answer: Send the bills to your carrier—to the organization selected by the Social Security Administration to handle medical insurance claims in your area.

Question: How are medical insurance benefits paid?

Answer: There are two ways, known as the assignment method and the payment-to-you method. Under the assignment method, which can be used only if you and your physician agree to it, your physician is paid directly. Your physician agrees also that his total fee will not exceed the reasonable charge. Medical insurance will pay him 80 percent of the reasonable charge and he will bill you for the remaining 20 percent and any of the $60 deductible you haven't met. In the payment-to-you plan, medical insurance pays 80 percent of your physician's reasonable charge directly to you, either before or after you pay your physician's bill, after deducting any of the deductible you haven't met. It's then up to you to pay the physician.

Question: If my physician and I agree to use the assignment method, how do we make the claim?

Answer: Use a form called Request for Medicare Payment (the form number is SSA-1490). You will fill out Part I of the form and sign it (your physician's office can help you). Then your physician will fill out Part II and send the form to the carrier for your area.

Question: How do I submit a claim if I decide to use the payment-to-you method?

Answer: Get a Request for Medicare Payment form, fill out Part I and sign it. Again, your physician's office can help you. Your physician will then either fill out Part II or give you an itemized bill. The bill must give date, place, description and charge for each service, the physician's name, your name and claim number and the diagnosis if possible. You then send the form, with either a completed Part II or the itemized bills, to the carrier for your area.

Question: How do I find out who my carrier is?

Answer: Your Social Security office can tell you. If you nonetheless send the claim to the wrong carrier, your claim will be forwarded to the right one. Remember to write the word "Medicare" in the carrier's address on the envelope, and include your return address.

Question: Right now I've got doctor's bills totalling about $40 for the year. Should I send them in now or wait until I've got enough to meet the $60 deductible?

Answer: You can do either. If you wait, as soon as your bills total $60 you should send them to your carrier. Your record will be marked to show that you have met the deductible for the year, and if any payments are due, they will be made to you. But since you said your bills now total $40, you may want to send them in now, so that when you send in your next bill—which is likely to put you over the $60 deductible—your record will already show that you've got $40 toward the deductible.

Question: I trust my carrier to keep my records straight. But maybe I should keep records of my own?

Answer: It's a good idea, because you might want to inquire later about any claims you have made. So keep track of the date you mailed your claim, the date, charge and nature of the services you received and the name of the physician or supplier.

Question: Is there a deadline for submitting claims?

Answer: Yes. If you received services between October 1, 1979 and September 30, 1980, your claim must be submitted by December 31, 1981. If you receive services between October 1, 1980 and September 30, 1981, your claim must be submitted by December 31, 1982.

Question: Where can I get the Request for Medical Payment forms?

Answer: From your Social Security office or, usually, at your physician's office. And each time you submit a claim, a new form generally will be mailed back to you.

Question: Will the Request for Medicare Payment form ask me a lot of complicated questions?

Answer: You'll have to give basics like your name, address, and sex, plus a description of the illness or injury for which you were treated. Be sure to give your name and claim number just as they appear on your health insurance card (and don't forget the letter at the end of your claim number!). And be sure to sign your name.

Question: What if I have someone else file the claim for me?

Answer: Whoever files for you should enter your name on the line that would ordinarily carry your signature, then write "By" and sign his own name and address. He should also tell his relationship to you and why you could not sign. Incidentally, he has only one line in which to write all this information so it's well to write small.

Question: Once I've met the $60 deductible, is it better to send in my bills as soon as I get them, or should I wait until a handful have accumulated?

Answer: The Social Security Administration suggests that you send in the additional bills as soon as you get them, since you'll be paid sooner that way.

Question: My bills are from several doctors. Do I have to use a separate payment-request form for each doctor?

Answer: No. The bills may all be sent with a single form.

Question: I know that I won't need to worry about submitting a claim with hospitals, skilled nursing facilities, home health agencies and other facilities participating in Medicare, because they submit the claim as a matter of course. But what if I get medical services and supplies from other sources? Who makes the claim then?

Answer: Either you or the supplier may do so, just as you would for physicians' bills.

Question: As a railroad annuitant, I'm not sure where I should send my medical-insurance claims. Can you tell me?

Answer: Send your claim—even if you are also entitled to Social Security benefits—to the Travelers Insurance Company office nearest your home, no matter where you received services.

Question: Please help me. My mother died before she had a chance to submit a claim for about $150 in doctor bills. What should I do?

Answer: You, or any other survivor, should contact your local Social Security office.

Question: Is it better to use the assignment method or the payment-to-you method in making claims?

Answer: Sometimes, the reasonable charge for a service, as determined by the carrier in your area, may be less than your physician's charge. In these cases, you may pay less if your physician agrees to the assignment method.

Question: The first time I submitted a claim, I used the payment-to-you method. Do I have to use this method all the time now?

Answer: No. You always have the prerogative of changing your mind.

Question: The amount paid on my claim looks wrong to me. What can I do about it?

Answer: Write to the carrier that handled the claim. If the carrier's explanation does not satisfy you and the amount in dispute is at least $100, you can request a hearing from the carrier.

Question: My physician refuses to use the assignment method. Can he do this?

Answer: Yes. In such cases, the payment will instead be made directly to you, whether or not you have paid the bill.

Question: I understand Medicare won't pay for the first three pints of whole blood (or units of packed red blood cells) I get. But will it pay for all blood after that?

Answer: It depends on whether the blood you get is covered under hospital insurance or medical insurance. Hospital insurance cannot pay for the first three pints you receive in a benefit period. The fourth pint and any others you receive *during the benefit period* will be fully paid for. Usually, if you receive blood under hospital insurance, it will be as a bed patient in a hospital. In contrast, medical insurance cannot pay for the first three pints you receive in a calendar year. However, the fourth pint and any others you receive, regardless of when in the year you get them, will be fully paid for. When you receive blood under medical insurance, it usually will be in physician's office, a clinic or the outpatient or emergency department of a hospital.

Question: Is there any way I can avoid having to pay for those first three pints of blood?

Answer: Yes—by arranging to replace them. You can do this by having a friend or relative donate the blood. Or maybe you belong to a blood-donor group that will replace the blood for you. Or perhaps your child or son- or daughter-in-law belongs to a blood-replacement plan that includes you as a beneficiary. If they do, you would be eligible for blood on the basis of their membership.

Question: I have both hospital insurance and medical insurance under Medicare. I was hospitalized for about a week and since then have had to use a number of the home health visits I'm entitled to under hospital insurance. Will these visits be counted against the 100 I'm also entitled to under medical insurance?

Answer: No.

Question: What if I need a physician or an ambulance while in a foreign country?

Answer: Your medical insurance can help pay for physicians' and ambulance services if they are done in connection with foreign hospital care that is covered by hospital insurance. Generally, hospital insurance covers services in a foreign hospital if you are in the United States and a foreign hospital is closer to you than is the nearest United States hospital that can give the care you need.

LIMITS OF MEDICARE

MEDICARE: A FAIRY GODMOTHER?

Unfortunately, Medicare cannot wave a magic wand and make all your medical bills disappear. Medicare is designed to help you out in a crunch. It was created to cope with serious, expensive situations. If you have to go to the hospital Medicare will pick up the tab for 60 days. Room, meals, nursing care, drugs—the works. In this kind of situation, Medicare really comes to the rescue.

But stay more than 60 days (or more than 20 days in a skilled nursing facility) and your expenses will skyrocket.

Medicare will not pay for nursing care while you recuperate. It will not pay for any drugs or other medicines. And medicine is expensive! And even though you carry Part B medical insurance your doctor's bills may outstrip Medicare payments because many doctors charge more than the "reasonable fee" designated by Medicare. Even though it will pay 80 per cent, the base figured allowed by Medicare may differ from the actual amount your doctor charges.

Always try to keep a rainy-day bank account just for medical emergencies, and definitely consider a backup health insurance plan.

Medicare is like a fairy godmother aiding you, but it cannot completely pave the way for you. Medicare is designed to cover the extremes. But it has no power to help in preventive medicine. A routine medical exam, for instance, which might turn up a problem before it becomes serious enough to warrant hospitalization, is not covered by either Part A or Part B of Medicare.

Even so, it's to your advantage to try to stay in good health and pay for your own check-ups at least once a year. Problems caught early are more easily and successfully treated than a full-blown medical crisis. And if routine physical examination should reveal a serious problem you can rely on Medicare to back you up.

THE LIMITS OF MEDICARE

Together Parts A and B of Medicare help pay for hospitalization, physicians' and surgeons' bills, care in a skilled nursing facility, home health care visits, treatment received in a hospital or in your doctor's office, and many more expensive medical expenditures.

But in spite of Medicare coverage, the average person over age 65 still pays at least half of his or her medical bills. It seems impossible, considering the billions of dollars in benefits paid out by Medicare every year, but it's true. Partly this is because elderly people need more medical attention, and thus have many more medical bills than younger people. And partly it's because there are many things Medicare does not cover. For instance, if your benefits run out before you leave the hospital, hospitalization can cost a king's ransom. And many people require convaslescent care after a stay in the hospital—and neither Part A or Part B of Medicare will touch these bills. And even if you carry Part B, your doctor's bills may still be far more than Medicare compensation.

MEDICARE DOES NOT COVER:

* Any hospital services once you have used up your 90-day benefit period or your 60-day lifetime reserve.

* Private nurses, nursing home or home care for general custodial care
* Drugs, even if they are prescribed by your doctor
* Routine physical exams
* Eye exams or eyeglasses
* Hearing exams or hearing aids
* Dental care or dentures
* Cosmetic surgery (unless required because of accidental injury or to correct a malfunctioning part of the body)
* Standard foot care (orthopedic shoes, etc.)
* Immunizations

THE MISSING PIECES

The biggest and most expensive gaps in Medicare benefits are private nursing care and drugs.

Nursing care can quickly demolish anyone's reserve funds. And drugs prescribed over a long-term, even lifetime, basis can erode one's basic weekly or monthly income. Often those who have to take drugs daily have to make genuine sacrifices of other necessities just to meet these bills.

SUPPLEMENTAL PLANS

Many people are turning to supplemental health insurance plans to take up the Medicare slack. If you are considering some additional insurance protection look for a policy that *fills in* Medicare's missing pieces at a reasonable cost. Foremost, you want a policy that covers private nursing care and drugs.

A supplemental policy should cover drugs, nursing care, mental health services, and as many other services missed by Medicare as possible.

Several prominent insurance companies offer health plans just for this purpose. These policies are designed to augment Medicare. They are usually available only to people age 65 or over who are also covered by Medicare. Blue Cross and Blue Shield, Mutual of Omaha, Travelers, Aetna Life and Casualty are only a few of the major insurance companies that offer supplemental health insurance policies. Their policies are not all the same; even the same insurance company may vary rates and coverage in different states. Check these and other plans in your state and compare them.

Shop and Compare

Surprisingly, different insurance companies may charge vastly different rates for similar policies. Allow yourself plenty of time for shopping around. You needn't grab the first policy you find. Some good policies have special enrollment periods, so it's a good idea to plan ahead.

Costs of supplemental plans vary, sometimes with legitimate reasons and sometimes with no reason at all. Usually costs depend on the extent of the coverage and the part of the country in which you live. Premium costs also depend on the amount of the deductible you are required to pay before the policy takes over. Remember, even the same company may vary rates and coverage in different states.

WHAT TO SHOP FOR

A good supplemental health insurance policy should pay all or part of the amount charged for the service, rather than giving you a set dollar-payment for each day (called indemnity payments). If a set dollar amount is paid you, say $60 a day, you will receive $60 a day no matter how high medical costs soar. But if you receive a *percentage*, as medical costs go up, your benefits also increase.

If you have indemnity benefits, medical costs could skyrocket but you would still get only a fixed dollar amount each day, which could be only a fraction of your actual medical costs, especially if you are in the hospital.

Look for a policy that fills in the largest number of missing Medicare pieces. Is there any chance the coverage will expand in the future? If so, will the additional coverage be offered to you as a supplemental to the basic benefits or will you have to purchase a new policy.

Also check the time limit for pre-existing illnesses. Will the policy cover an illness you already have? You should be able to find a policy that covers any existing illness up to six months before you apply. That is, if you broke your leg two weeks before you took out the policy, you would be covered for any medical costs incurred by the broken leg. But if you had a heart problem six months or longer before you signed up, and subsequently needed any care associated with your heart condition, you would not be covered.

Avoid duplicating your Medicare benefits. If your supplemental policy offers the same benefits as Medicare, you're wasting your money. They won't both pay.

Be cautious of mail order insurance that offer cash benefits after 60 days in the hospital. Most people never stay in the hospital for 60 days. Usually if you are ill for a long period your doctor will try to move you to an extended care facility. You will probably never see those cash benefits.

Also, in many instances, mail order insurance requires that you be a policy holder for as long as two years before you are eligible to collect benefits; others exclude specific health conditions. Look at these policies very carefully, and make sure that the company is licensed by your state.

HEALTH MAINTENANCE ORGANIZATIONS (HMOs)

When you belong to a Health Maintenance Organization, a monthly fee entitles you to full health care, from physical exams and drugs to operations and nursing care. Many people find an HMO a compatible fit with their Medicare coverage because HMOs emphasize preventive medicine.

The main advantage of this kind of plan is that HMO doctors routinely accept Medicare assignments. You can visit the doctor whenever you need to and all treatment and checkups are covered by the same basic monthly fee. This means that problems are often caught early. On the whole, while people who belong to an HMO tend to use the service more, they spend fewer days in the hospital and in the long run visit the doctor less than other people the same age.

Health Maintenance Organizations usually have standard arrangements to receive direct payment for services covered by Medicare. Some only receive direct payment under Part A (hospital insurance), and others under Part B (medical insurance). Some receive direct payment for both.

If you are interested in an HMO find one closely tied to Medicare so your bookkeeping is kept to a minimum. The idea of an HMO is to make your life easier, not more complicated. Even if the HMO is closely aligned with Medicare there may still be some services offered by Medicare that you do not receive through an HMO. In those instances, you will need to collect for these services directly from Medicare.

HMO's are not cheap, but most participants use the services frequently. The disadvantage is that you are not able to select your own doctors or hospital. You must use those provided by the HMO to which you belong. Very often, of course, this is really an advantage because many excellent health facilities are maintained by HMOs in different parts of the United States. But you would want to investigate the HMO facilities in your immediate vicinity carefully before deciding to take the plan.

Before making a decision about an HMO try to talk to other people you know who belong. Are they satisfied with the plan? Is the membership growing? Inquire about the medical facilities and the staff. In other words, does the HMO have a good reputation? Is it near your home? (This could be a prime consideration if you must make frequent visits to the doctor or hospital.) Does the HMO provide home health service? Emergency service? Convaslescent service? Cost-wise, does the HMO compare favorably with other plans? If the answer is yes to all or most of these questions, then an HMO may be the plan for you. You can ask at your Social Security office for information about HMO's in your area.

HELP FROM MEDICAID

If you are covered by Medicare, but cannot pay for all the medical services that Medicare misses, Medicaid can help you. If you can't pay your medical bills, even though you have some income, Medicaid can help pay your Medicare premiums and deductibles, and your share of medical costs. You do not have to be on welfare to receive Medicaid, but you do have to be in need.

Medicaid can help pay for hospital services, physicians' services, diagnosis and treatment for people under age 21, home health care, skilled nursing services and many other services.

Medicaid programs are run by the state and they are not part of Medicare. If you need help and think you might qualify, you can check with your hospital or call your nearest Medicaid office (listed in the telephone book under *Medicaid Information*).

ADDITIONAL NOTES AND SPECIAL CASES

MILITARY SERVICE CREDITS

Military service counts towards your Social Security benefits. But if you have served in the Armed Forces you may have earned some extra credits that will increase your Social Security benefits when you reach retirement age. These extra credits do not show up on your earnings statement. You must tell Social Security that you have been in the service and give them the dates. If it turns out that these extra credits would give you a higher benefit, Social Security will ask you to supply your service record.

Military service prior to 1957 usually cannot be used towards both Social Security and military pensions.

If you saw active military duty between September 15, 1940 through 1956, you may be awarded additional earnings credits of $160 a month.

If you were on active military service from 1957 on, your basic pay counts toward Social Security. But you can receive extra credits of $300 for each calendar quarter that you served up to 1977. If you served from 1978 on, you can receive extra earnings credits of $100 for every $300 of annual military salary covered by Social Security to a maximum of $1,200 credits for the year.

VETERAN'S BENEFITS

People who have served in the Armed Forces are eligible for all VA benefits—even if they are also insured under Social Security. Social Security protection does not preclude VA benefits except in one instance.

Even if you collect Social Security, you may still be entitled to receive veteran's benefits as well. If you are a veteran insured by Social Security here are some of the VA benefits you might be eligible for:

Compensation for a service-connected disability.

Pension for *non-service* related disability if you are a veteran of either World War, Korea, or Vietnam.

Life insurance.

Business and farm loans.

Housing loans.

Mortgage insurance.

Vocational rehabilitation if you are disabled.

Hospitalization. (First priority for admission goes to veterans who require treatment for disabilities incurred or aggravated in military service. Also eligible, as space permits, are honorably discharged veterans who are unable to pay the cost of medical care. Any veteran over 65, or any veteran receiving pension, will be admitted regardless of his ability to pay.) You can apply directly to a VA hospital, outpatient clinic, regional office or through any veterans service organization.

Eligible veterans can also receive medical and dental services, medicines, and medical supplies on an outpatient basis. These services are available in VA facilities or authorized private physicians in your area. Eligible veterans would include those who have a disability incurred or aggravated in service, those entitled to vocational rehabilitation, and all military retirees.

Survivor's Compensation. Death compensation and pensions are paid to survivors of servicemen who died on duty or from a service-connected cause.

Widows. If a serviceman died in World War II, his widow may be entitled to Social Security. Even if he never worked under Social Security he may have earned enough extra military credits to entitle his survivors to Social Security. Check with your Social Security office to see if you qualify.

How to Apply

The VA Veterans Assistance Personnel provide information and assistance on all benefits legislated by Congress. Phone or visit the nearest VA regional office or Veterans Assistance Center for information.

Remember that you may receive extra Social Security work credits if you were in the service for certain periods. When you file any claim for Social Security be sure to mention your military work record.

***The VA also provides a pension for needy survivors of veterans who died in service but whose deaths were not due to service. These special payments are made only if the veteran was *not insured by Social Security*. If he was covered by Social Security, his survivors will be eligible for Social Security benefits.

HOUSEHOLD WORKERS

In most jobs, Social Security contributions are taken from your pay automatically. But this may not be the case with household workers. Household workers have to pay careful attention to their income to make sure they are getting Social Security work credits.

Household workers include babysitters, maids, cooks, laundry workers, butlers, gardeners, chauffeurs, and people who do housekeeping or repair work—anyone employed in or around someone else's home.

If you are a household worker and you earn cash wages of $50 or more—including cash transportation expenses—in a three-month calendar quarter, your wages are covered under Social Security. That means that in each calendar quarter you must receive cash wages of $50 or more from one employer before you pay into Social Security. The employer must file a quarterly return and also give you an earnings statement every year. Cash wages do not include food, clothing, tokens for buses or subways, or other non-cash items.

You should show your employer your Social Security card and tell him or her to deduct Social Security contributions from your wages. If you don't, you won't get Social Security credit for your work. And if you don't have enough Social Security credits, you and your family won't be able to get monthly benefits on your wage record when you retire or if you become disabled or die.

If you are a household worker and have several different employers it would be to your benefit to make sure that at least one of them meets this requirement every quarter.

If You Employ Household Workers

If you employ a household worker, it's your job to see that wages you pay are properly reported. You must deduct Social Security contributions from wages, pay an equal amount as the employer, and send them to the Internal Revenue Service with a report of total wages paid.

You can get help with the correct forms at your Social Security office or the office of Internal Revenue Service.

COUNTING YOUR TIPS

Many working Americans receive a large portion of their wages in tips. This is fine for the time they are working. But when they reach retirement age they often find that their Social Security benefits are low because a large part of their income was unrecorded.

If you earn more than $20 a month in tips (with one employer) you should definitely include it in your Social Security contributions. Keep track of the tips you earn and submit a written statement to your employer at the end of the month. Your employer can pay your Social Security tax by deducting it from your wages, or he can pay it with money you give him for that particular purpose. Or you can make the payment yourself by sending the contribution directly to the Internal Revenue Service.

What if your tips are considered part of your wages? Some jobs pay less than the minimum wage because you earn tips that are supposed to make up the difference. In this case, your tips are actually part of your cash wages. According to the present law your employer must pay his share of the Social Security contribution on tips which are counted as part of your wages.

FARM WORKERS

Farm workers follow slightly different guidelines for Social Security insurance. If you work on a farm or ranch you need to earn at least $150 a year from one employer before you can get Social Security credits. If you are paid by the hour, day, or week (instead of by the piece) you must work 20 or more days for cash wages in a year.

Migrant farm workers who are allowed to temporarily work in the U.S. on a seasonal basis are not covered by Social Security.

CLERGYMEN

Priests, rabbis, and ministers have a choice about Social Security. They can decide not to pay Social Security self-employment tax on their earnings. But if they do exercise this option, they are automatically excluded from collecting Social Security benefits when they retire. However, if they do pay self-employment Social Security tax, they are entitled to the same benefits as any other worker insured under Social Security.

WORKING ABROAD

If you decide to combine work and travel abroad, pause long enough to consider your position vis-a-vis Social Security. In the long term you may be losing tremendous benefits by working in a foreign country. Foreign companies, unless they are in business in the U.S.A., don't contribute to the American Social Security system. And if you work for a foreign company abroad, you will not pay into the Social Security system either. In fact, you might be required to pay into that country's pension plan—and may never have the opportunity to collect.

Even if you work in the overseas branch of an American company you can still miss out on Social Security credits. American companies operating abroad are subject to several complex tax and business laws that often prohibit American employees abroad from earning Social Security credits.

Usually if part of your salary is payable in the United States, at least that part will be taxed for Social Security and you will earn Social Security credits . . . but you will probably earn less credits than you would receive if your entire salary was counted.

However, if you work for a foreign-owned company in the United States, you are on sure ground as far as Social Security is concerned. You will pay into Social Security and receive credits just as if you were working for an American company. The guideline is if you receive your pay in the United States or if you are paid in a foreign country. However, the method of reporting your earnings will vary from the traditional mode if you work for a foreign government office.

Working for a Foreign Government

A special rule applies to the United States citizen who works in this country for a foreign government, an international organization, or an instrumentality wholly owned by a foreign government.

You must report your earnings from these employers as though you were *self-employed*. You include a separate Schedule-SE with your Federal income tax return and pay Social Security self-employment taxes on your earnings.

FOREIGN WORKERS IN THE UNITED STATES

Aliens who are lawful permanent residents of the United States carry a Registration Receipt Card (Form I-551) with them at all times. Any services performed as a permanent resident are covered by Social Security on the same basis as services performed by other employees.

An alien should explain his or her immigrant status to his employer. Social Security status should also be discussed with the employer and, if necessary, with the Social Security office to determine if the work is covered.

FOREIGN STUDENTS AND EXCHANGE VISITORS

More than 200,000 foreign students and exchange visitors enter the United States each year to study, lecture, or engage in other academic work. Many bring their families.

For the most part, foreign students and exchange visitors are not allowed to work for pay or engage in business unless they receive special permission.

If such permission is granted, Social Security contributions are *not* withheld from wages because the services are considered as part of the purpose for which the student or exchange visitor was admitted.

If the person works without permission, contributions *must* be withheld if the work is covered under Social Security.

Income taxes are generally withheld from earnings even when Social Security contributions are not.

Reporting Earnings

Contributions *are not withheld* and earnings are not reported for Social Security if (1) the nonresident alien is working and has the permission form from the Immigration and Naturalization Service, (2) has a letter from a sponsor granting permission to work, or (3) is a foreign student doing on-campus work.

Contributions *are withheld* and earnings reported if the nonresident alien is working without permission, and the employment is covered by Social Security.

Foreign Students

A foreign student is a nonimmigrant alien temporarily admitted to the United States to study at a school, university, or other recognized institution approved by the Attorney General. Status is F-1 on the student's Arrival-Departure Record.

In general, a foreign student can only work in this country if specific permission is granted by the immigration authorities. For example, he may receive permission if the employment is recommended by the school for practical training in the student's field of study. Or if employment is financially necessary.

If permission is granted, the student's earnings are exempt from Social Security.

In most cases, a foreign student does not need special permission from the Immigration and Naturalization Service to work on campus.

The spouse or children of students are classified F-2, and they are *not* permitted to work. However, should they perform work illegally, all services are covered by Social Security and contributions will be withheld.

Exchange Visitors

An exchange visitor is a student, scholar, trainee, teacher, professor, research assistant, specialist, leader in a field of specialized knowledge or skill, or similar person temporarily admitted to this country to participate in an exchange visitor program designated by the secretary of state. Status is J-1.

An exchange visitor generally may work for the same kinds of reasons as a foreign student. Written permission to work is given in a letter by the sponsoring program. Earnings are not covered for Social Security and no contributions are withheld.

The spouse or children of the exchange visitor are classified J-2 and can work only with the permission of the immigration authorities. Should they work without permission, all services are covered and Social Security contributions are withheld.

If you need information about immigration and naturalization matters, call the Immigration and Naturalization Service office in your area.

RAILROAD WORKERS

Railroad workers have their own retirement system that is unrelated to Social Security. These workers are covered by the Railroad Retirement Act (RRA) which pays retirement, disability, and survivor benefits in much the same way that Social Security does.

But sometimes people who work for the railroad also have other jobs in their lifetimes. In that case, they may be covered by both Social Security and the RRA.

If a railroad worker has done other work which was covered by Social Security, that work is credited to a separate Social Security account. It's possible then when he retires to receive benefits from both programs.

If most of his credits are with the railroad, his additional Social Security credits can be transferred to boost his railroad retirement. If most of his work is under Social Security, his railroad credits can be transferred to raise his Social Security benefits.

He may even be fully insured under both programs if he has earned enough credits in each. In that case, he can actually receive two pensions (although his railroad pension will be slightly reduced.)

The wife of a railroad worker can also receive dependent's benefits from both plans. If she is fully insured for Social Security on her own, she gains an advantage with a combined RRA dependent's benefits and her own Social Security benefits.

A railroad worker can also apply extra military credits towards either RRA or Social Security benefits, whichever gives the greatest advantage. But this is not done unless he makes a special request to Social Security or the Railroad Retirement Board.

If you are a railroad worker and thinking of getting another job to work under Social Security, check first with your Railroad Retirement Board. If you actually leave the railroad for another job, you break what is called your "current connection" with the railroad. You may lose some of your potential benefits by doing this. However, it is all right to work both jobs at the same time, or to earn money through self-employment. Check first.

UNEMPLOYMENT COMPENSATION AND SOCIAL SECURITY

It's possible to collect Social Security and Unemployment Compensation at the same time. Let's say you are eligible for Social Security. Perhaps you are 62 or over and still working. Or perhaps you collect other Social Security benefits besides retirement. If you lose your job you can still apply for Unemployment Compensation. If you have been collecting reduced Social Security benefits while you work, notify Social Security that you've lost your job so they can restore your full benefits. You do not have to tell them you are applying for Unemployment Compensation.

All workers whose employers contribute to state unemployment insurance programs are eligible for Unemployment Compensation. Federal civilian employees and ex-servicemen are eligible if they are unemployed, registered and ready for work, and meet the earnings requirement of the state law. Benefits are usually paid on a weekly basis for 26 weeks. When unemployment reaches specified levels on a state or national level, benefits are extended for up to an additional 26 weeks.

If you find another job your Social Security benefits may drop again, depending on your new salary. If you are between 65 and 72, you can earn $5,500 a year without losing any benefits. If you are between 62 and 65, you can earn $4,080 a year. If you earn more than these amounts, you will lose $1 in benefits for every $2 you earn. Of course, if you are over 72 years of age, you can make as much money as you like without losing a penny of your Social Security benefits. (As soon as you go back to work, however, your Unemployment Compensation will stop.)

COAL MINERS AND BLACK LUNG BENEFITS

Coal miners who are disabled because of pneumoconiosis (black lung disease) are entitled to monthly cash benefits to replace their lost income. Widows of miners who died of black lung disease may also receive benefits; if no spouse survives, children are entitled to receive the benefits.

To be eligible for payments, a miner must be totally disabled from black lung disease, meaning that he can no longer work in the mines, although he may be able to work outside the coal mine.

Black lung benefit provisions of the Coal Mine Health and Safety Act of 1969 are administered by the Social Security Administration. For information or to apply, telephone or visit your local Social Security office.

WORKMEN'S COMPENSATION AND SOCIAL SECURITY

If you are in a situation where you are eligible for Workmen's Compensation at the same time you are collecting Social Security, you can collect both.

Most states have Workmen's Compensation laws, although they do not apply to every job. In some states the law covers only employees in hazardous jobs or companies with a large number of employees. But if your job is protected by Workmen's Compensation you will receive medical and cash benefits if you are injured on the job.

For example, if you continue to work after age 65 and are injured on the job, you can collect both Social Security and Workmen's Compensation, as long as the two together do not add up to more than 80 per cent of your usual salary. (*Note:* You cannot collect Social Security disability benefits because disability ends when you reach retirement age.)

OTHER INCOME

In most all cases, the only income you have to worry about is money you *earn* on the job. You can receive almost any other kind of money along with your Social Security—pension, Workmen's Compensation, Unemployment Compensation, VA benefits, public assistance, dividends, tax refunds, inheritances, and so on. None of these sources of income will affect your Social Security benefits.

MEDICAID AND SOCIAL SECURITY

Medical assistance in the form of Medicaid is available to people who do not qualify for Medicare. Even people who have Medicare but cannot afford all the deductibles, premiums, and their share of medical expenses that Medicare doesn't pay can apply for help from Medicaid. And you do not have to be covered by Social Security to be eligible.

Usually those people who are eligible for Supplement Security Income are also eligible for Medicaid. Even if you earn more than the SSI allowance, you may still qualify. People with very little money receive Medicaid free. Those with low-incomes (not enough to meet medical bills) usually pay a small premium.

Remember, you don't have to be on welfare to get medical assistance from Medicaid. Nor do you have to be covered by Social Security.

Medicaid is funded by both federal and state governments. But each individual state runs its own program. Unfortunately, there have been many cases of abuse and fraud—by the public, by officials, and by doctors. Even so, there are still many good Medicaid programs and many good doctors who treat Medicaid patients fairly and with concern.

Here are some of the benefits you might receive if you qualify for Medicaid:

Hospital service—both inpatient and outpatient

Skilled nursing home services

Home health care

Physicians' services (home, office, or hospital)

And many other services available to younger family members such as family planning (you don't need to be over 65 to receive Medicaid services). Age restrictions vary depending on the service required.

Again, even if you receive Medicare and Social Security, you may still be able to get assistance from Medicaid to help make up for the missing pieces Medicare does not pay for. For information, call your nearest Medicaid office, listed in your telephone directory under *Medicaid*, or check with your nearest public assistance office.

SOCIAL SECURITY AND PENSIONS

Most people fortunate enough to have a pension plan will be able to collect their pension along with their Social Security benefits when they retire. One does not exclude the other. When you pay into Social Security you are entitled to collect your benefits regardless of how much other income you may have (except income earned on a job).

A few people, however, are on the spot. There are some retirement plans that deduct Social Security benefits. This means that your pension check will never increase with the cost of living. For example, say your pension plan pays you $850 every month. But your Social Security benefits check of $300 is subtracted from that amount. You still receive $850—but your pension plan only pays a fraction of the total amount: $550. Your Social Security benefits are likely to increase over the years, but your monthly income will always stay the same. Because as Social Security goes up, your pension plan goes down. This is obviously not the kind of retirement plan you want to have, and if you have a choice, try to join a different plan, one that is completely distinct from Social Security.

GOVERNMENT PENSION OFFSET

Dependents' Social Security benefits paid to spouses, widows and widowers may be reduced by the amount of any pension or annuity that person receives based on work in non-covered public employment. This provision is effective for benefits paid for December 1977, based on applications filed in that month or later.

However, the offset does not apply if the spouse, widow or widower would be eligible for public pensions before December 1982, as long as they also qualify for Social Security dependent's benefits under the law in effect on January 1, 1977.

TAX ADVANTAGES

All Social Security benefits are free from taxation. Since you are *not* required even to claim Social Security income on your income tax form, your benefits cannot put you in a higher income bracket. This is true for local, state, and federal taxes. Social Security benefits are free and clear.

Money you receive from Medicare cannot be taxed, either. Nor do you have to report the money Medicare sends you to help pay medical bills on your income tax.

However, any money you *pay out* for premiums, deductibles, and your share of medical bills is *tax deductible*. Be sure to claim those expenses under "medical deductions" on your income tax statement.

QUESTIONS AND ANSWERS: SPECIAL CASES

Question: Is the time I spent in the Armed Forces covered by Social Security?

Answer: Yes. Social Security credits of $160 are given for each month of active duty between September 14, 1940 and December 31, 1956; credits of $100 are given for each month of active duty between January 1, 1957, and December 31, 1966, and credits of $100 plus basic pay are given for each month of active duty after January 1, 1967. If you are in the 1940-56 group, the credits will not be listed on your earnings record, but don't let this stop you from claiming them if they would affect the size of your benefits. Just remember to bring proof of your military service when you apply. If you are in the 1957-66 group, or if you are a survivor of someone who was, you should tell your Social Security office, since this period until recently was not included in the law. If you are in the post-1967 group, your credits are subject to a maximum of $9,000 for 1972; $10,800 for 1973 and $13,200 for 1974; $14,100 for 1975; $15,300 in 1976; $16,500 in 1977; $17,700 in 1978; $22,900 in 1979; $25,900 in 1980, and $29,700 in 1981.

Question: I served in the Armed Forces in the 1940-56 period, but was dishonorably discharged. Do I still get Social Security credits?

Answer: No.

Question: I saw active duty in the Armed Forces in the 1940-56 period, but for only 90 days. Is that long enough for Social Security?

Answer: Yes, but with nothing to spare. Veterans of 1940-56 have to have served at least 90 days to get credits, unless a condition caused by or aggravated by their military service forced them to be released sooner.

Question: Are civil servants covered by Social Security?

Answer: Employees of state and local governments are covered if the state or local government and the Federal government have made an agreement. Most Federal employees not covered by a staff retirement plan are covered by Social Security.

Question: I am a clergyman. How does Social Security affect me?

Answer: If you are a clergyman—that is, if you are an ordained, commissioned or licensed minister, a Christian Science practitioner or a member of a religious order who has not taken a vow of poverty—earnings you have received since 1968 will be covered automatically unless you file an application directing otherwise. You probably know that before 1968, clergymen who wanted to be covered had to sign an application saying so. These clergymen will not be affected by the new rules—their coverage will continue.

Question: Why would a clergyman decline to be covered?

Answer: Some clergymen say that for reasons of conscience or because of religious principles they are opposed to receiving Social Security benefits for their work.

Question: Once I decide I don't want my earnings as a clergyman covered, can I change my mind?

Answer: After you have filed your application, it cannot be withdrawn.

Question: I'm planning to work abroad. Can I still be covered by Social Security?

Answer: Yes, if your employer abroad is American or if you are going to work aboard vessels or aircraft of foreign registry. If you will be working for a foreign subsidiary of an American company, you will be covered if the company agrees with the Secretary of the Treasury that Social Security contributions will be paid for all United States citizens employed abroad by the subsidiary.

Question: As a typical student with the typical student's money problem, I'm eager to keep my benefits coming as long as possible. I know the checks will stop the year I reach 22—will anything besides growing older end my student benefits?

Answer: Yes, and here's a crash course: Your checks will stop if you marry, quit school or cut attendance to less than full time.

Question: Is Social Security available to people who work for nonprofit organizations?

Answer: Yes, if both the organization and the employees who want to be covered file a form with the Internal Revenue Service and if the organization is operated exclusively for religious, charitable, scientific, literary, educational or humane purposes, or if it conducts tests for public safety. The organization must file form SS-15, waiving its exemption from making Social Security contributions. The employees must file form SS-15a. Employees who are hired or rehired after the calendar quarter in which the forms are filed will also be covered. If any employee earns less than $50 prior to 1978, $100 from 1978 on, his wages for that quarter will not be covered.

Question: I'm in the United States temporarily under a foreign-exchange program. Will any work I do be covered by Social Security?

Answer: As a foreign national, you will not have Social Security payments deducted from your paychecks (1) If you have permission from the Immigration and Naturalization Service to work, or (2) you have a letter from your sponsor granting you permission to work, or (3) you are a foreign student doing on-campus work.

Question: My grandchildren won't accept my wisdom but they would like to accept benefits based on my earnings record. It would be nice if they could—how can they?

Answer: Grandchildren can collect if they are living with a

SPECIAL CASES 173

grandparent and were getting at least half their support there during the year before the grandparent became disabled, became entitled to retirement or disability benefits or died. They can collect if they lived with a grandparent before they were 18. They can collect if they were living with the grandparent at the time he became disabled, became entitled to benefits or died. And they can collect if they are adopted by the surviving grandparent after the working grandparent dies and if their natural or adoptive parent was not living with the grandparent and making regular payments for their support when the grandparent died.

Question: An acquaintance of mine, an illegitimate child, jokes about how illegitimate children have been denied thrones, respect, inheritances, etc. What about Social Security benefits?

Answer: In 1972 the United States Supreme Court ruled that an illegitimate child had as much right to Social Security benefits earned by his father as legitimate children had. The decision overturned the Social Security policy of giving illegitimate children a smaller share of a dead father's survivor benefits, or sometimes no benefits at all. Now, all offspring will share equally. In 1973, a three-judge panel in Washington, D.C., overturned a law barring benefits to illegitimate children born after the father reached age 65. The law had limited benefits to children who could establish their paternity before the father became 65.

Question: Does a child still run the risk of losing his benefits if he is adopted by a distant relative or by someone not related to him?

Answer: No. At one time, a child lost his benefits if adopted by other than certain relatives. Now, children collecting benefits continue to collect no matter who adopts them. If a child's checks were stopped under the old regulation, he can get back payments to October, 1972, by reapplying.

Question: How does the law apply to household workers?

SPECIAL CASES

Answer: Household workers get Social Security coverage if their cash wages (not food, clothing, subway tokens or other non-cash items) paid by one employer total $50 or more in a calendar quarter. The employer should make sure the prospective worker has a Social Security number, and he must file quarterly returns in addition to giving the worker a yearly earnings statement. The local Social Security or Internal Revenue Service office can help provide these forms.

Question: What if my household help and I decide not to make our Social Security payments?

Answer: This is against the law.

Question: I'm a Japanese-American who was ordered into an American "concentration camp" during World War II. Is it true I can get Social Security credits for this?

Answer: Yes. United States citizens of Japanese ancestry can get free wage credits for the time they were interned during the war and were 18 years old or over. You should apply for these credits if you think they could increase your monthly benefits.

Question: A fellow coal-miner says I can collect benefits because I got black-lung disease. Is that right?

Answer: Yes. The black-lung benefit provisions of the Coal Mine Health and Safety Act of 1969 is administered by the Social Security Administration. Information is available at your Social Security office.

Question: Part of my earnings are in the form of tips. Do they have to be included when my Social Security contributions are figured?

Answer: Yes—if the tips amount to $20 or more a month with one employer. You can pay the Social Security contributions due on these tips in two ways. You can give your employer a written report of your tips within 10 days after the end of the month in which you receive them. Your employer will then pay your contribution out of your wages or with money you give him for this purpose. Or, you can pay the contribution directly to the Internal Revenue Service. Employers who pay an employee up to 50 per cent less than the Federal minimum wage if the employee receives tips that make up the difference between actual pay and the minimum wages now must pay the employer's share of the Social Security contribution on tips which are counted as wages for the purposes of the minimum wage law.

Question: Are migrant workers covered by Social Security?

Answer: No. (Migrant workers here means foreign workers admitted to the United States on a temporary basis for farm work.)

Question: We railroad workers have our own Railroad Retirement Board. Does this affect the Social Security Administration's policy toward us?

Answer: Yes. Your earnings from railroad work are reported, not to the Social Security Administration, but to your own board, which also pays the benefits for railroad work you've done. Your railroad work will not be entered on your Social Security record. However, if you retire or become disabled with less than 10 years—120 months—of railroad work, your railroad earnings after 1936 will be considered when your Social Security benefits for disability or retirement are computed.

Question: I guess I've got a foot on both sides of the tracks. I've worked more than 120 months on a railroad, and I've also done enough nonrailroad work to qualify for Social Security benefits. Can I collect from both the Railroad Retirement Board and the Social Security Administration when I retire? And when I die, can my family collect from both?

Answer: Since you've worked long enough "on both sides of the tracks" to qualify for both programs, you can indeed receive two sets of retirement benefits. But when you die, your survivors will be able to collect from one program only. However, all of your earnings—your railroad work after 1936 and your work under Social Security—will be considered when the payments to your survivors are calculated.

Question: My husband and I never got around to a wedding ceremony, but we've lived together as a "married" couple for 30 years. Now he's approaching retirement and I'm wondering if, as his common-law wife, I will be eligible for wife's benefits and Medicare.

Answer: It depends on whether you've lived in states that recognize common-law marriages. Twelve states now do—Alabama, Colorado, Georgia, Iowa, Kansas, Montana, Ohio, Oklahoma, Pennsylvania, Rhode Island, South Carolina and Texas, plus the District of Columbia. These states require that the couple be free of other ties and that they make an informal but definite agreement to consider themselves married. In addition, some states require that the couple acknowledge their marriage in some public way—spreading the word among acquaintances or opening joint charge accounts as "Mr. and Mrs.," for example.

Question: I'm a farm worker (not a migrant). Do I qualify for Social Security?

Answer: If you work for a farmer, ranch operator or farm-labor crew leader, you are covered by Social Security if you get cash wages from one employer of $150 or more in a year for farm work, or if you do farm work 20 or more days in a year for cash wages paid on the basis of time, rather than by the piece.

Question: I'm a household worker employed on a farm. Does that make me a household worker or a farm worker? The reason I ask is that I understand the Social Security rules are different for household workers than for farm workers.

Answer: If you are employed on a farm or ranch operated for profit, you are considered a farm worker governed by the rules given directly above. Otherwise, you are considered a household worker and must earn at least $50 in cash wages from one employer in a calendar quarter to earn Social Security credits.

Question: The problem with serving many masters! I do seasonal farm work and sometimes have a hassle at income-

SPECIAL CASES

tax time trying to get my earnings records from all the people I work for. Exactly what are my employers supposed to give me in the way of wage information?

Answer: If you earn $600 or more in a year for farm work for one employer, the employer must give you a Wage and Tax Statement (a W-2 form). If you earn less than $600, your employer must give you a statement of earnings, which doesn't have to be a W-2 form. Because some employers might forget, it might help to keep track of all your employers' names and addresses. You could call it your master list.

Question: How can farmers, farm operators and ranchers get Social Security credits?

Answer: You must have net earnings from self-employment of $400 or more in a year and must report these earnings in your income-tax return. If you gross $600 to $2,400 in a year from farming, you can report two-thirds of the gross, instead of the net, for Social Security purposes. If you gross more than $2,400 and your net earnings are less than $1,600, you can report the actual net of $1,600 for Social Security purposes. If the gross is more than $2,400 and the actual net is over $1,600 you must report the actual net.

Question: Can I get Social Security credit for the income I get from renting farm land?

Answer: Yes, provided you "materially participate" in the production on the farm or in the management of the production.

Question: I'm self-employed and have been paying into Social Security right along. But it looks like my shop is going to have to be closed next year for renovations and more modern equipment. Is there any way I can keep adding to my Social Security credits even though I expect to lose money next year?

Answer: Yes. For taxable years after 1972, whenever your earnings are less than $1,600 and less than two-thirds of your gross nonfarm income, you can report the two-thirds of your nonfarm income—up to $1,600—as your Social Security creditable income. However, you can do this only five times, and only if you are regularly self-employed.

Question: My wife has three children from an earlier marriage who are fully supported by their real father. Will they also be eligible for my Social Security benefits if I should die?

Answer: Yes—if you were married to their mother for at least nine months (or at least three months if your death is accidental or related to military service). If the children live with you, it makes no difference who supports them. If they don't live with you, you would have to provide at least half of their support if they are to qualify for your survivors' benefits.

Question: We swear this is a serious question, not some joke. We are two homosexual men who have been living together as a married couple for many years. We even got a sympathetic homosexual minister to perform a wedding ceremony for us. Both of us have been working under Social Security. Because of our different physical builds and temperaments, one of us considers himself the "wife" and the other the "husband." When one of us retires, gets injured or dies, will the other be able to collect a wife's or husband's benefits?

Answer: At this writing, the Social Security Administration had no formal rule regarding homosexual marriages. A staff worker at a New York office said decisions probably would have to be made on a case-by-case basis.

OTHER QUESTIONS AND ANSWERS

Question: Can I work and get Social Security benefits at the same time?

Answer: Yes. If you are between the ages of 65 and 72 you can earn up to $5,500 per year (under 65 the amount is $4,080 per year) with no reduction in your benefits. Of course, you are free to earn as much as you want to or are able to, but $1 in benefits may be withheld for every $2 you earn beyond the above amounts. However, in the year you retire, your full benefit will be paid for any month in which you do not earn more than $459 per month if you are 65 or over or $340 if you are under 65 and do not perform a substantial amount of self-employed work. Social Security regulations define "substantial" as 45 hours' work a month or more, although in some cases the figure may be as low as 15. Your Social Security office can tell you what applies in your case.

Question: I am 72 years of age, what can I earn?

Answer: You can earn any amount without affecting your benefit. In 1982, you will be able to earn any amount when you are 70 years of age.

Question: Can I draw welfare benefits as well as Social Security benefits?

Answer: Yes, provided that you can meet the requirements set down by the city, county or state that runs the welfare program you are interested in. Welfare programs are operated by local governments, not by the Social Security Administration, so qualifying for one program may or may not qualify you for the other.

Question: I'm already collecting Social Security benefits. Can I also get food stamps?

Answer: Possibly. It depends on what your income is. The United States Department of Agriculture has begun an effort, called Project FIND, to inform aged Americans about its food-assistance programs. More information is available from the department's local offices.

Question: My widowed grandmother is living with her boyfriend—age 76!—out of wedlock. She says their combined Social Security benefits are higher this way than they would be if they got married. Is this possible? And advisable?

Answer: Your grandmother can now decide upon marriage based on factors other than reduced widow's benefits. As of January, 1979, there is no loss of benefits if a widow or widower remarries after the age of 60.

Question: I had been collecting benefits as a dependent wife ever since my husband's retirement. Now we're divorced. I'm planning to remarry, but my fiance, who thinks of everything, wants to know if I would lose my benefits.

Answer: If you were over age 62 when your divorce became final and you were married at least 10 years, you would not lose your benefits. If your husband-to-be collects benefits too, the Social Security Administration, which also thinks of everything, says you can collect on the basis of whichever husband had the highest earnings.

Question: A friend says that a man with a nonworking wife and a house full of dependent children should be getting a fortune in benefits when he retires. Or is there a limit on how much one family can collect?

Answer: There is a limit, ranging from $229.70 to $1,143.70, depending on the man's earnings and the age at which he retires.

Question: What does the Social Security Administration think of nepotism? I'm planning to employ some members of my family.

Answer: It depends on whether you plan to employ your

parents or your progeny. Any work done by a parent for a son or daughter's trade or business is covered by the law. Domestic work done by a parent in a son or daughter's home is not covered unless special conditions are met. Work done for a parent by a child under 21 years of age is not covered, whether that child is a son, daughter, stepchild, adopted child or foster child. Nor does the law cover work done by a wife for a husband or by a husband for a wife.

Question: My husband and my friend's husband have roughly the same salary. But I work and my friend is "just a housewife." Who is going to come out ahead when we all reach the golden years? Will my friend's benefits as a dependent wife outweigh my own benefits as a wage earner? Would I have been smarter not to bother working?

Answer: A wife who has never worked a day in her life can, upon reaching age 65, collect half of what her husband gets in retirement benefits. So the answer depends on how much you and your husband earn. For example, if your husband and your friend's husband both are eligible for $266 a month when they retire, your friend could collect half of that—$133—when she reaches 65. And if you as a working woman earned an average of $1,760 a year, you would collect your own retirement benefit of about the same amount—$135. If you earned under $1,760 a year, obviously your retirement benefits would be less than your friend's benefits. But if you earned more than $1,760—which wouldn't be unusual—you would collect more than your friend. Of course, $1,760 is not the universal cut-off point. It only applies when the husband's retirement benefits are $266. But there is a general rule: If neither partner in a marriage earns the maximum amount on which Social Security taxes are based (the maximum now is $29,700) but their joint salaries equal the maximum, they may be paid less in total retirement benefits than another couple having the same total earnings, but where only the husband works.

Question: I'm a divorcee. I'm told I can draw benefits on my former husband's earnings if I can prove he provided half my support. How do I do that?

Answer: You no longer have to. Whether you are a divorced wife, a divorced widow or a divorced mother, if you are at least 62 and were married for at least 10 years, you can collect as soon as your former husband retires and draws benefits.

Question: I will be 62 in 1981. Will my benefits be figured differently?

Answer: Yes. Those people who reach age 62 in 1979 through 1983 will have their benefits figured using a new method in which the actual earnings will be adjusted to take into account changes in average wages since 1951. These adjusted earnings will be averaged together and the benefit rate figured from this average. You will receive the higher of the two benefit rates resulting from computing your benefit with the usual method used and this new way.

Question: What is the average Social Security benefit?

Answer: The average benefit for a retired worker is $330.00 while an aged couple receives $563.00. An aged widow receives $310 while a disabled worker with his wife and children receives a family benefit averaging $728.00. Remember that these amounts are averages and that benefits vary from a low of $153.10 to a high of $653.80 for a 65-year-old retiree.

INDEX

additional earnings
  (after retirement), 37, 179
addresses, change of, 30
addresses, Social
  Security, 11
age, 28, 33, 180, 182
appeals, 31
applying for Social
  Security:
  delayed, 29
  how, 9, 29, 34
  if denied, 31
  when, 28, 33-34
  where, 13
benefits:
  additional earnings,
    and 39
  average payment, 182
  computing, 24-26, 38
  maximum, 22, 27, 39
  minimum, 22, 27, 39
  rates, 36, 38
  requirements for, 24
  when working, 179
  who receives, 33
black lung benefits,
  165, 174
blind workers, *see* disabled
cards, Social Security:
  application for, 9
  name change, 11
  replacement, 10
  stolen, 10
changing jobs, 30-31
cheating, 12

children:
  adopted, 173
  disabled, 33, 63-64,
    67, 95
  illegitimate, 173
  students, 33, 79, 172
clergymen, 160, 171
coal miners, 165
common-law marriages, 176
confidentiality, 4-5, 10
contributions,
  percentages, 7-8
cost of living raises, 2, 9
creditors, 29
credits, *see* work credits
currently insured, 24
delayed application, 28
delayed retirement credit,
  23, 38
dependents, 28, 40, 180
  see also husbands, wives,
    children
depression era, 1
direct deposit, 5, 30
disability benefits:
  appeals, 59-60
  applying for, 45, 56,
    58-59
  back payments, 63
  dependents and, 46-47,
    53, 59
  eligibility for, 4, 43,
    46, 62, 67
  how long, 46, 54, 61-62
  how much, 46, 49, 55-57

if working, 45, 50, 61
military, 67
and other SS benefits,
  49-59, 60, 63
who collects, 53
work credits required,
  44, 54-55
disabled people:
  definition of, 43, 50,
    53-54
  disabled blind, 43-44,
    55, 64-65
  disabled children, 33,
    46, 54, 59, 63-64, 67
  disbled survivors,
    47, 62, 65
  disabled widows & widowers,
    47, 66
  Medicare, 48, 68, 106
  rehabilitation, 51-52,
    60-61
  renewal disability, 62-63
  trial work periods, 62
  Workmen's Compensation,
    48, 65
divorced spouses,
  benefits, 40
documents, *see* records
earnings, taxable maximum,
  20-21
eligibility:
  application, 9
  not covered, 2-3
  personal records required,
    5-6
  time periods, 14
  how much work, 24
  see also work credits
family employees, 180-181
farm workers, 160-162
farm & ranch operators,
  177
food stamps, 82, 179-180
foreign-government
  employees, 20, 160

foreign students, 162-163,
  172
foreign travel, 30
foreign workers in U.S.,
  161, 175
Fuller, Ida, 2
fully insured, 3, 24-25
funding, 1-2, 7
government employees, 171
government pensions, 168
grandchildren, 42, 172
household workers, 158,
  173-174
husbands:
  applying for benefits, 35
  eligibility, 4, 33, 41
  how much, 40
  self-employed, 19
  see also survivors
ineligible for Social
  Security, 2-3
information, 12
investment income, 39
Japanese-Americans, 174
jobs covered, 9
joint ventures, 20
kidney disease, 49,
  101-104, 108
living together, 176, 178
lost checks, 29-30
Medicaid, 155, 166
Medicare, 105-155:
  age, 99, 105
  applying, 33, 117-118, 132
  benefits periods, 110,
    116-117
  buying Medicare coverage,
    98, 107, 118
  Christian Science
    sanatoriums, 123
  compared w/ private
    insurance, 98, 128
  deductibles, 135
  dental care, 139
  dependents, 98

INDEX

disabled, 106
eligibility, 96-97, 105, 117-118
emergency cases, 140
enrollment, 100
expenses paid, 109-110, 115
foreign hospitals, *see* outside U.S.A.
funding, 106, 119
government employees, 101
health facilities, 107, 119, 129
Health Maintenance Orgs., 153-154
home health care, 113, 122, 126, 140-141
hospital services, 109-124, 126
kidney disease, 101-104, 108
limits of, 149-151
Medicaid, 155
medical insurance, 125-148
mental health benefits, 120, 128
not covered, 106, 118
nursing care, 112, 121
other protection, 149, 151
outside U.S.A., 107-108, 123, 148
Part A, 109-124
Part B, 97, 125-148
payments, receiving, 124, 144
physicians & surgeons payments, *see* Part B
premiums, 134
reasonable charges, 130-31, 135-36
w/out Social Security, 98, 107
submitting claims, 144-145
supplemental plans, 151-155
taxes, and, 104
women, and, 100
Workmen's Compensation,
 and, 104
military service, extra credits, 16, 156, 170
death benefits, 78
disability, 67
moving, 30
numbers, *see* cards
offices, Social Security, 11
payments, receiving, 31, 35
pension plans, 9, 27, 167
quarters, 24, 26
railroad workers, 20, 163, 175
 Medicare, and, 146
records:
 checking on, 11-12
 earnings, 13-14
 personal, required, 5-6, 29, 34
 where kept, 11
rehabilitation, vocational, 51, 60-61
remarrying, 180
retirements, attitudes toward, 32
retirement plans, 39, 27
Roosevelt, Franklin D., 1
savings, 8
self-employment:
 applying for benefits, 34
 estimating, 19
 income tax, 19
 net earnings, 17
 options, 18
 receiving credit, 177
 reporting earnings, 18
 spouses, 19
 see also joint ventures
  foreign-government
  employees,
  farm and ranch
  operators
spouses, *see* husbands *and* wives
Social Security:

INDEX

application, 9, 13, 28, 33-34
compared to savings, 8
computing benefits, 24-26
contributions, 7-8
delayed retirement, 23
how funded, 7
increases, 29
maximum earnings, 20-21
other retirement plans and, 27
refunds, 21
retirement and, 3
taxes, 21
work covered, 9
Social Security Act, 1, 7
statement of earnings, 13-14, 21-22
stolen cards, 10
stolen checks, 29
students, 33, 79, 172
Supplemental Security, 81-95:
 AFDC, 81
 appeals, 89-92
 applying for, 95
 disability and, 94
 eligibility, 83, 86, 94
 food stamps, 82, 179-180
 how much, 84, 93
 income limitations, 83, 94
 property limitation, 83, 94
 receiving payments, 84-85
 reporting, 86-87
 SSI, 82
survivor's benefits, 4, 28, 69:
 applying, 77
 as insurance, 69-70, 73-74
 children, 75-76, 79, 178
 deferred payments, 71
 disabled, 47, 62
 divorced, 65, 72, 73
 eligibility, 70, 75-77
 lump sum payments, 71-72
 Medicare for, 73
 military, 77
 parents, 78
 remarried, 72, 80
 when, 76
 widows & widowers, 72-73, 76, 80
 work credits required, 78
taxes, Social Security, 21-22, 168-169
tips, counting, 159, 174
unemployment compensation, 164
veteran's benefits, 157
welfare and Social Security, 179
wives, dependent:
 applying for benefits, 35
 divorced, 40-41, 65, 180-181
 eligibility, 4, 33
 how much, 40
 remarried, 41, 180
 see also survivors
wives, working, 42
 self-employed, 19
 see also, survivors
work credits:
 computing benefits, 24-26
 defined, 15
 extra, 27
 how earned, 3, 14
 how many, 15, 26-27
 military credits, 16
work, returning to:
 age, 28, 35
 how much you can earn, 35-36, 39
working abroad, 160, 171-172
working plus benefits, 179
Workmen's Compensation:
 disability benefits and, 48
 Medicare and, 104
 Social Security and, 166

25399

HD Andrews, David
7125
.A56 Your rights to social
security benefits

CHAMPLAIN COLLEGE LIBRARY